SECOND EDITION

Word
Pocket Guide

Walter Glenn

Beijing · Cambridge · Farnham · Köln · Paris · Sebastopol · Taipei · Tokyo

Word Pocket Guide, Second Edition
by Walter Glenn

Copyright © 2004, 2002 O'Reilly Media, Inc. All rights reserved.
Printed in the United States of America.

Published by O'Reilly Media, Inc., 1005 Gravenstein Highway North,
Sebastopol, CA 95472.

O'Reilly & Associates books may be purchased for educational, business, or
sales promotional use. Online editions are also available for most titles
(*safari.oreilly.com*). For more information, contact our corporate/
institutional sales department: (800) 998-9938 or *corporate@oreilly.com*.

Editor:	Brett Johnson
Production Editor:	Reg Aubry
Cover Designer:	Emma Colby
Interior Designer:	David Futato

Printing History:

November 2002:	First Edition.
April 2004:	Second Edition.

0-596-00684-5
[C]

Contents

Part II. Word Tasks

Part III. Word Reference

Part IV. Word Resources

Word Pocket Guide

Introduction

This updated Word Pocket Guide covers the most recent versions of Microsoft Word—Word 97, 2000, 2002, and 2003. It includes lots of useful information for both new and experienced users in a quick and easy-to-read format. The guide is divided into four sections:

- Part 1 provides an overview of the most important concepts in Word. You will learn how to navigate the Word interface, load and use templates, format documents, and solve the most common Word complaints. By gaining a deeper understanding of how Word operates, you will be able to work more efficiently.

- Part 2 shows you how to tackle specific tasks covering every aspect of the program, including formatting, spelling, editing, printing, customizing Word's operations and interface, and more. It also digs into features specific to Word 2003, such as Reading Layout view, XML, Shared Workspaces, and Research Services.

- Part 3 contains a number of reference tables listing keyboard shortcuts, regular expressions, and common file locations. You will learn how to perform sophisticated searches using wildcards and special character codes, as well as how to use built-in key combinations to select text, format characters, and work with tables.

- Part 4 lists Internet sites that offer useful tools, utilities, tips, and tricks.

Conventions Used in This Book

The following typographical conventions are used in this book:

Italic
> Indicates new terms, URLs, filenames, file extensions, directories, and program names. For example, a template filename might look like this: *Normal.dot*.

`Constant width`
> Is used to show the contents of files, commands and options, or the output from commands. For example, you might read, "At the command prompt, type `winword.exe` to launch Word normally."

Constant width italic
> Shows typed text that should be replaced with user-supplied values. For example, type ***filename*** into the File name box and click the Open button.

Menus/Navigation
> This book uses arrow symbols to signify menu instructions. For example, "File → Print" is a more compact way of saying, "Click File on the command bar at the top of the screen and choose Print from the drop-down menu." However, if an instruction directs you to click a tab, check an option, or click a button in a dialog box, we'll tell you. For example, to print draft output, select File → Print, click the Options button, and check the Draft output box.

Pathnames
> Pathnames show the location of a file or application in Windows Explorer. Folders are separated by a backward slash. For example, *C:\Program Files\Microsoft Office* means the file being discussed is in the Microsoft Office subfolder of the Program Files folder.

This icon highlights an especially cool or useful feature in Word. Even Word experts might learn a thing or two, or be reminded about an old favorite trick.

In Part 2, the following icons appear in the margin next to certain tasks:

03+

This icon indicates the features are only available in Word 2003.

02+

This icon indicates the features are only available in Word 2002 and later versions. Word 97 and Word 2000 do not incorporate these features.

00+

This icon indicates the features are available in Word 2000 and later versions.

If no icon is present, the features are available in Word 97, 2000, 2002, 2003, and later versions.

Understanding Word

The first part of this book covers the principal functions of Word. It helps new users hit the ground running and provides experienced users with a keener understanding of how Word works.

This part of the book covers:

- The Word Interface
- Template and Document Files
- How a Document Works
- Formatting
- Shortcut Menus
- What Word Tries to Do for You
- The Most Common Word Complaints

NOTE

Except where indicated, the information in this chapter applies to Word 97, 2000, 2002, and 2003.

The Word Interface

Microsoft has changed some of the features and overhauled much of the underlying technology over the years, but the basic Word interface looks much the same.

Figure 1 shows the important elements of the Word 2003 interface. Numbered items in this list correspond to the labeled elements in the figure.

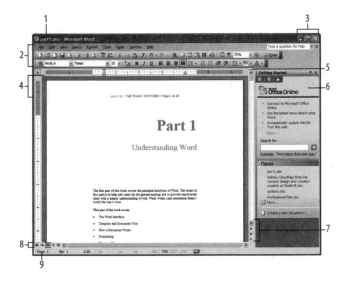

Figure 1. The Word 2003 interface

1. *Title Bar.* This bar shows the name of the document and the document's state. For example, if you open multiple windows of the same document (Window → New Window), Word labels the documents *:1* (the original), *:2*, and so on. If you open a document as read-only or as a copy, this designation appears in parentheses beside the document name.

2. *Command Bars.* Word calls menus and toolbars command bars. You can add buttons, commands, and even submenus to any command bar (see Part 2). A feature named *adaptive menus*, enabled by default in Word 2000-2003, causes Word to show only the basic commands (as decided by Microsoft) and frequently used commands on

a menu, unless you click an extra button to show all commands. To disable this feature, select Tools → Customize, click the Options tab, and check the Always Show Full Menus box (in Word 2000, disable the Menus show recently used commands first option).

Word 2003 offers over two-dozen built-in toolbars. The program only shows the Standard and Formatting toolbars by default, although others appear based on your actions. For example, when you create a table, the Tables and Borders toolbar turns on automatically. Select View → Toolbars to toggle common toolbars on and off. Select Tools → Customize and click the Toolbars tab to see the full list of available toolbars.

3. *Window Controls*. These controls work a bit differently, depending on whether you use a single or multiple document interface. In the single document interface, you see a separate window and taskbar button for each Word document. In the multiple document interface, you see all Word documents in one master window.

  • In the single document interface, the Minimize, Maximize, and Close buttons on the titlebar affect only the active document. If only a single document is open, Word adds a separate Close Window button to the far right-hand side of the menu bar. Click this button to close the document, but leave Word open. Use the regular Close button on the titlebar to close both the document and Word.

  • In the multiple document interface, the Minimize, Maximize, and Close buttons on the titlebar affect the master Word window and all documents open inside it. Word adds Separate Minimize, Maximize, and Close buttons to each document window.

4. *Rulers.* Two rulers (horizontal and vertical) control the
   margins and indentation of text in a document. The
   horizontal ruler (see Figure 2) appears directly above the
   main document window in all of Word's views, except
   for Outline view. The vertical ruler appears on the left,
   but only in Print Layout view. For the most part, the
   vertical and horizontal rulers behave the same way,
   except the vertical ruler lacks tabs.

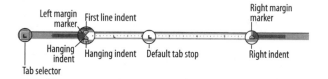

Figure 2. Rulers control tabs, indentation, and margins

Click the tab selector button at the far left in the ruler to
cycle through the available tab types. Left, center, and
right tabs indicate how text is aligned on the tab. Decimal tabs align numbers on the decimal point. Bar tabs
create vertical display lines. Indents control the placement of the first line and hanging indents (which you can
also adjust by dragging the ones already on the ruler).
Once you select a tab type, click anywhere on the ruler to
place a tab.

Drag the light gray dividers (called margin markers) between the white space and shaded space on the ruler to adjust the printable margin of the page.

5. *Screen Split Handle*. Double-click this handle (or drag it down) to split the document window into two separate panes, allowing you two views of the same document. Changes you make in one pane appear instantly in the other. You can also drag selections between panes. Double-click the handle again (or drag it all the way to the top) to close the extra pane.

6. *Task Pane*. Task panes (available in Word 2002 and 2003) group collections of tools and commands related to a particular task. Task panes are arguably more efficient than dialog boxes for certain tasks because you can continue to view and work in your document while managing tasks in the pane. Task panes open automatically, depending on context. For example, when you select File → New, the New Document task pane opens with tools for creating and finding documents. While a task pane is open, click the title of the pane to drop down a list of available panes.

NOTE

Some third-party vendors make task panes that you can download. For example, the Amazon Research Pane lets you perform Amazon searches within Word and insert the bibliographic (or sales) information directly into a document. You can download the Amazon Research Pane at *http://www.amazon.com/gp/associates/research-pane/download_rp.html/104-2490312-0238357*.

---

7. *Browse Object*. This group of buttons let you browse through different objects in a document. Click Select Browse Object (the round button) to specify how you want to browse. You can browse by field, endnote, footnote, comment, section, page, edit, heading, graphic, or table. Once you select a browse object, use the Next and

Previous double-arrow buttons to jump from object to object in a document.

8. *View Buttons*. These buttons provide fast access to Word's five primary views:

   • *Normal* provides a larger workspace, but does not accurately display margins or other page setup configurations. An advantage to Normal view is that it uses horizontal lines to make page and section breaks more visible. It also inserts text in the line (such as "Page Break") to indicate the type of break.

   • *Web Layout* shows any background color or graphic (Format → Background) added to the page. It also shows the positions of text and graphics as they would appear in a web browser. Word 97 calls this the Online Layout view, but it works pretty much the same way.

   • *Print Layout* adds an extra vertical ruler on the left-hand side of the page. It also displays the physical edges of the paper, which is useful when laying out a document and monitoring pagination.

   • *Outline* displays the document as a hierarchical list of headings and supporting paragraph text. You can use this view to plan and structure document headings.

   • *Reading Layout* (introduced in Word 2003) displays two pages side-by-side using Microsoft ClearType, a font-smoothing technology that uses wider margins, larger font sizes, and other formatting tricks to make reading documents on your computer screen easier. Reading Layout is handy when reading a document quickly, but it's difficult to use when making changes.

9. *Status Bar*. Word's status bar at the bottom of the page (see Figure 3) shows the location of the current view in a document (by page) and the location of the insertion point from the top of the page (by section number, page count, line, column, and distance).

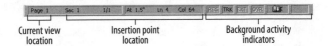

Current view location   Insertion point location   Background activity indicators

Figure 3. The status bar displays your location in a document and any background activity

The status bar also indicates certain settings and background tasks. It lets you know when:

- Word is recording a macro (REC)
- The track changes feature is on (TRK)
- Extended double-click is on (EXT)
- Overtype is on (OVR)

Icons also appear on the status bar when Word repaginates, spell-checks, or saves a document.

NOTE

Double-click the REC, TRK, EXT, and OVR icons to toggle the selection on or off.

Template and Document Files

Word uses four primary types of files:

- Word creates and names a *document file* (.doc) whenever you save a new document. Documents contain text, formatting information, styles, macros, fonts, embedded graphics, and customizations to the Word interface. Word can also open other types of document files—such as rich-text files (*.rtf*) or text files (*.txt*)—but these do not have all the functionality of a Word document.
- A *template file* (.dot) contains all the same elements as a document, and can also hold formatted AutoText entries (see Part 2 for more on AutoText). Template files hold

collections of styles, customizations, and boilerplate text and associate those collections with documents. Every document has at least one template attached to it. Word bases new blank documents on the *Normal.dot template*, but you can base a document on any template. You can also attach a template to an existing document to make the template's collection of styles available (select Tools → Templates and Add-Ins and click the Attach button). You can only attach one template to a document at a time.

NOTE

From Windows Explorer, double-click a template (*.dot*) file to create a new document with that template attached to it. Right-click the template file to open the actual template or to perform other options. Find out more about using templates in Part 2.

- Word creates one *temporary file* (*.tmp*) when you open an existing document or save a new document for the first time. This *.tmp* file is very small—usually only 1KB in size. Word marks the *.tmp* file as hidden in Windows Explorer and gives it almost the same name as the main document file. Word replaces the first letter of the filename with a tilde (~) and the second with a dollar sign. Word uses this file to track changes you make to an open document. It stores the *.tmp* file in the same directory as the open document and discards it when you close the document. Unfortunately, Word uses this file mostly as "working space." You can't really recover any meaningful information from it if Word crashes.

NOTE

Word often leaves this small *.tmp* file lying around (after a crash, for example). Word uses this temporary file to determine the state of a document, so if a document won't open or save, look in the document's folder for a leftover *.tmp* file and delete it. This is less of a problem in Word 2002 and 2003, which support automatic document recovery.

Each time you save an open file, Word creates an additional *.tmp* file in the same directory as the document (therefore, if you've saved a document three times since opening it, there will be a total of four *.tmp* files). The .tmp files created on each save are different from the small *.tmp* file discussed previously in two ways. First, they are essentially copies of the document at the save point and are nearly identical in size to the main Word document. Second, the files are not named after the document, but have a sequential naming pattern (usually something like ~WRL1620.tmp). While these *.tmp* files contain useful information, they are not much use in a crash because you will have already saved the document (that's when the files are created). They can be useful, though. If you save your work periodically, you can, if necessary, return to a previous version of your document a few save points back. Simply copy the *.tmp* files to another location before you close the current document (otherwise Word will clear away the files), and then open the version you want.

- If you enable the AutoRecover feature (select Tools → Options, click the Save tab, and check the Save AutoRecover info every *x* minutes box), Word creates an AutoRecover file whenever you open a document. It updates the AutoRecover file at a specified interval. In the event of a crash, you can usually recover the most recent update merely by restarting Word. You can find a list of locations where Word stores AutoRecover files (and other common files) in Part 3.

NOTE

Word can also open, create, and save other types of files, including *.html*, *.xml*, and several text file formats. Support for other types of file formats depends on the converters installed on your system.

How Templates Are Loaded

Word loads its interface—menus, toolbars, commands, styles, keyboard shortcuts, and so on—in layers each time you start the program. The complete interface or *global layer* is built in the following manner:

1. When you start Word, the program files begin to build the framework for the interface—including basic menus and toolbars.

2. Word loads a global template named *Normal.dot*, which contains styles and customizations you have made to the Word interface—custom menus, keyboard shortcuts, and so on. These customizations override the interface elements created in step 1.

3. Word loads any template files (those ending in *.dot*) located in the various startup and template folders. (For a list of locations, see Part 3.) Any customizations or features in these template files override or add to the interface features built in steps 1 and 2.

4. At this point, Word is done—but you can tweak even more. To load additional templates manually, select Tools → Templates and Add-Ins and click the Add button. The Templates and Add-Ins dialog box also lets you remove templates and lists all currently loaded templates. You can also create or load documents to add yet more templates.

So why should you care how templates work? First, if you understand how Word loads templates and builds its global layer, you can identify and alter the behavior of specific templates. For example, let's say a style you saved to *Normal.dot* is not working the way you think it should. Another template may be overriding it with a style of its own that has the same name. Taking a brief tour through the loaded and attached templates may help identify the source of the problem.

Second, templates store a lot of good information. If you record a macro, create a style, or customize the Word interface, you must save your changes to a template or document. If you save them to *Normal.dot* (the default choice most of the time), your changes appear in all documents. If you save them to a different template, you must load the template or attach it to a document to access items in the template.

Finally, templates are a powerful tool for customizing and automating your work. You can create templates that contain boilerplate text, predefined styles, customized menus, and even macros. Custom templates are a great way to standardize documents and streamline their creation. For example, you could create a template of a letter with text you use regularly. When you create a new document from the template, the boilerplate text appears and you just "fill in the blanks."

NOTE

To launch Word in safe mode, type word.exe /a at the command prompt or in the Run dialog box. In safe mode, *Normal.dot*, templates in the Startup folder, add-in libraries, and user settings stored in the Registry are not loaded. Safe mode is a good way to open documents that otherwise won't open due to problem macros or other settings. See Part 3 for details on other ways to start Word.

Tips on Using Templates

The following tips help you work with templates and documents in Word. You'll find advice on performing other template-related tasks in Part 2.

- *Normal.dot* is the most important template. Word saves all customizations, styles, macros, and so on to it, unless you specify another template. Word also stores any AutoCorrect entries with formatting and all AutoText entries to *Normal.dot*. You can copy the template to other computers to carry your settings with you. The table of common file locations in Part 3 shows you where Word stores the *Normal.dot* template on different kinds of systems.

- Any customizations, styles, etc. applied to the current document override those found in loaded templates, which in turn override settings found in *Normal.dot*, which in turn override those loaded by default in Word. Confused? Consider the following example. You assign the Ctrl-Shift-D key combination to the Paste Special command and save it to the *Normal.dot* template. The key combination now works in any open document (unless another template overrides it). If, however, you were to save the key combination to a template besides *Normal.dot*, it would work only in documents attached to the template. Finally, if you were to save the key combination in a document, it would work only in that document.

- When you right-click a Word document in Windows Explorer, the shortcut menu lets you open the file, print it using the default printer settings in Word, or view the file's properties. The properties include the filename, type, location, and size, as well as the date you created, last modified, and last accessed it. The shortcut menu for template files offers the same options. Select New from the shortcut menu to create a new document based on the template.

- The Word documentation mentions several kinds of templates, including global, user, and workgroup templates. The implication that there are different kinds of templates is misleading. All templates are really the same; only their use differs. Word adds global templates when it starts up (specify them through Tools → Templates and Add-Ins). Word stores user templates on a user's computer and attaches them when you create a new document. Workgroup templates are loaded in the same way as user templates, but Word stores them on a network server.

- You can create various types of documents (Legal Pleadings, Letters and Faxes, Memos etc.) based on templates. These document types are based on templates that Word saves (by default) in the main Templates folder (see Part 3 for details on common file locations). If you save a template to the Templates folder, you can access it through the File → New command.

- When you create a document based on a template (or attach a new template later), Word copies all of the styles, macros, and other goodies to the document file. If the template contains an item (style, macro, etc.) with the same name as an item in the document, Word replaces the item in the document. To automatically update the same items in both the document and template, select Tools → Templates and Add-Ins and check the Automatically update document styles box.

How a Document Works

Every Word document consists of a main text layer sandwiched between front and back drawing layers (see Figure 4). The main text layer contains text, inline objects, and framed objects. The front and back drawing layers contain floating objects and are like transparencies laid on top of and under the text layer of a document. The combination of all three layers represents the final document.

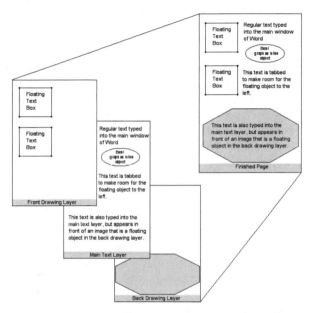

Figure 4. The layers of a document

The main text layer contains the bulk of a document. It holds text and two other types of objects:

- *Inline objects* appear in line with the text. An inline object is treated like a character. The insertion point moves over an inline object just like it moves over a character. Text does not wrap around inline objects. With the exception of text boxes and drawing objects (WordArt, Charts, etc.), Word inserts all objects (inserted pictures from files, clipart, etc.) as inline objects by default.

NOTE

You should use inline objects when you need the object to behave like a character. For example, you might want to format the object using tabs and indents, or apply paragraph and character styles.

- *Framed objects* have a frame around them (which may or may not be visible) that affects the way text flows around the object. Framed objects are really a holdover from very early versions of Word (pre-Word 97) that did not have drawing layers. Floating objects, discussed next, rendered framed objects obsolete.

When the front and back drawing layers were added to Word, a third type of object became available—floating objects. As the name implies, you can place floating objects anywhere on a page and move them around without regard to the position of text in the main text layer. This works because floating objects do not exist in the main text layer. Instead, they reside in either the front drawing layer (and thus appear in front of the text) or the back drawing layer (and appear behind text). When you use Word's *format* object command to send objects to a position in front of text or behind text, you are really choosing the drawing layer on which they should appear.

You can even stack floating objects on top of one another within a drawing layer. For example, suppose the back drawing layer contains a background graphic for a newsletter and a text box with an advertisement. If you stack the two objects, the graphic appears behind the textbox. This creates an additional layer effect, even though both objects live on the same drawing layer (see Figure 5).

Floating objects are either anchored or unanchored to a particular paragraph. An anchored object moves when the paragraph moves. An unanchored object stays when the paragraph moves.

Figure 5. Stacking floating objects within a layer

NOTE

When you edit a document, select Tools → Options, click
the View tab, and check the Object anchors box to view
anchors. Use the Print Layout view to get an idea of how
images will look in a printed document.

You can choose whether text should wrap around a floating
object (as it would with a framed object) or whether it
should be shown on top of or beneath the text (depending on
which drawing layer it's in). To do this, select the object and
choose Format → Object and click the Layout tab. The command *Object* in your Format menu may vary, depending on
the actual type of object selected (i.e., Picture, AutoShape,
etc.).

Word 2002 and 2003 add a new drawing element called a
canvas. Essentially, a canvas is a grouping tool that collects
all the floating objects on a single layer. This means you can
have two drawing canvases—one in the front drawing layer
and one in the back drawing layer. The canvas groups
objects so you can move them together and apply a common

border and background. A separate frame around the object represents the canvas. You can remove objects from this canvas by dragging them off of the canvas and you can delete the canvas itself (without deleting the objects in it) by selecting the canvas and pressing Delete. To prevent Word from creating canvases, select Tools → Options, click the General tab, and check the Automatically create drawing canvas when inserting AutoShapes box.

NOTE

Three additional layers create headers and footers in a document. These additional layers (known as the header/footer layers) live behind the back drawing layer. Any objects or text in the main drawing or text layers always obscure objects and text in the header/footer layers. It helps to think of the header/footer as a separate document behind the main document.

Formatting

Regardless of how you think your document is constructed (words form sentences, which form paragraphs, which form pages, etc.), Word sees all documents as having three parts:

- A document has one or more *sections*.
- A section has zero or more *paragraphs*.
- A paragraph has one or more *characters*.

Word has three types of formatting, each named for one of the three parts of a document.

Sections

Sections are the largest piece of a document to which you can apply formatting. While Word's interface often makes it seem as if you can apply formatting to an entire document or

---

specific pages, you are really just applying formatting to sections of a document.

Sections control the page formatting and flow of a document (by forcing page and column breaks). All new documents are created with one section, which contains everything you type, unless you do one of the following:

- Select Insert → Break to manually insert a section break. Adding sections lets you vary the layout of a document within a page or between pages. For example, you could use different margins on the title page, body, and appendix of a document. You could also vary the way header items, such as page numbers, appear on odd and even pages.

  There are three types of section breaks. A Next page break starts a new section on the next page. A Continuous page break starts a new section without starting a new page. An Even or Odd page break starts a new section on the next odd or even page.

- Change the formatting (orientation, margins, page layout, or page numbering, for example) on a range of pages, a single page, or even part of a page. In this case, Word automatically creates a new section. Remember, Word doesn't really see pages—only sections. If you want finer control of the layout process than Word provides when automatically creating sections, take the time to plan the document layout first and create the sections yourself. You almost always get a better result.

NOTE

By default, section breaks appear only in Word's Normal view and show up as dashed horizontal lines. To display section breaks in other views, select Tools → Options, click the View tab, and check the Hidden text box.

Paragraphs

The ultimate success of every bit of formatting in a document depends on the paragraph. In Word, a paragraph consists of a paragraph mark (¶) and all of the text preceding that paragraph mark up to, but not including, the previous paragraph mark or the beginning of the document (see Figure 6).

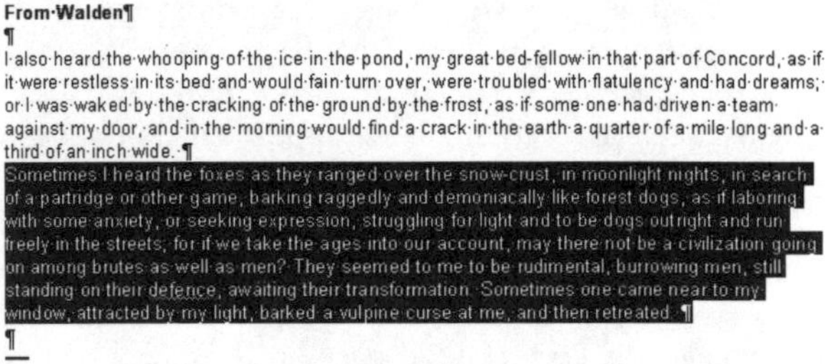

From·Walden¶

¶

I·also·heard·the·whooping·of·the·ice·in·the·pond,·my·great·bed-fellow·in·that·part·of·Concord,·as·if·it·were·restless·in·its·bed·and·would·fain·turn·over,·were·troubled·with·flatulency·and·had·dreams;·or·I·was·waked·by·the·cracking·of·the·ground·by·the·frost,·as·if·some·one·had·driven·a·team·against·my·door,·and·in·the·morning·would·find·a·crack·in·the·earth·a·quarter·of·a·mile·long·and·a·third·of·an·inch·wide.·¶

Sometimes·I·heard·the·foxes·as·they·ranged·over·the·snow-crust,·in·moonlight·nights,·in·search·of·a·partridge·or·other·game,·barking·raggedly·and·demoniacally·like·forest·dogs,·as·if·laboring·with·some·anxiety,·or·seeking·expression,·struggling·for·light·and·to·be·dogs·outright·and·run·freely·in·the·streets;·for·if·we·take·the·ages·into·our·account,·may·there·not·be·a·civilization·going·on·among·brutes·as·well·as·men?·They·seemed·to·me·to·be·rudimental,·burrowing·men,·still·standing·on·their·defence,·awaiting·their·transformation.·Sometimes·one·came·near·to·my·window,·attracted·by·my·light,·barked·a·vulpine·curse·at·me,·and·then·retreated.·¶

¶

Figure 6. Selecting a whole paragraph, including the paragraph mark

---

NOTE

To create a well-formatted document, you need to see paragraph marks. You can click the Show/Hide button on the Standard toolbar, but this button also turns on many other hidden characters, such as spaces and tabs. If you find them too distracting, select Tools → Options, click the View tab, and use the options in the Formatting marks section to turn on specific formatting characters.

The paragraph mark

The paragraph mark is a character. It has a font, size, and color just like other characters. You can move, copy, and even delete paragraph marks. They contain all the character and paragraph formatting information for a paragraph. The number of paragraph marks equals the number of paragraphs in a document. Every time you press the Enter key, Word creates a new paragraph mark.

What makes a paragraph mark special?

- It holds all the formatting information for the paragraph, including character formatting—fonts, sizes, style, color, indents, outline level, bullets, and tabs.

NOTE

You can't adjust a paragraph's format by selecting the paragraph mark and applying new formats directly to it. This action just applies character formatting to the paragraph mark itself.

- It marks the end of a paragraph. No text may be typed after the paragraph mark. Using the right arrow to move over it causes the insertion point to move to the beginning of the next paragraph. The End key jumps to the end of any line. If the line contains a paragraph mark, it jumps to a position right in front of the mark.
- The final character in a document is always the paragraph mark. Word associates a wide variety of formatting with the final paragraph mark, especially section and style formatting.

Tips on using paragraphs

- When you hit Enter, Word creates a new paragraph mark (and thus a new paragraph). To define the formatting style applied to the new paragraph, select Format → Style, click the Modify button, and choose a style from the Style for following paragraph drop-down menu. By default, the new paragraph uses the same style as the previous paragraph. Styles are covered later in this part.
- You can select a paragraph in three ways: click and drag to select all the text in the paragraph (or in multiple

paragraphs), triple-click anywhere in the paragraph, or double-click in the margin to the left of the paragraph. If you use the click-and-drag method, make sure you select the paragraph mark as well. Once selected, you can move or copy the paragraph to a new location and keep its formatting intact.

- If you want to select only the text in a paragraph and not the paragraph mark, try the following: click to the left of the paragraph mark and then click at the beginning of the paragraph while holding down the Shift key. You can then move or copy the text to another location (e.g., an existing paragraph) without carrying over the formatting or creating a new paragraph.

Characters

Characters are the smallest elements of a document. You can select and apply a different format to a single character in a word, a single word in a paragraph, or even a blank space. Formatting you can apply directly to characters includes font, font size, font style, character spacing, and special text effects.

Word inserts a character every time you press a non-navigational key. Some characters appear as printable text, others as non-printing characters. Tabs, returns, spaces, page breaks, and section breaks are all non-printing characters in a document. You can select, move, or delete them just like any other character. Click the Show/Hide button on the Standard toolbar to display these non-printing characters in a document (see Figure 7).

Styles

A style is a collection of formatting information. Word recognizes two types of styles:

Figure 7. Paragraph marks, tabs, and space characters appearing in Show/Hide mode

- *Paragraph styles* can include both paragraph formatting (such as tabs, line spacing, and indenting) and character formatting (such as font, size, and color).

- *Character styles* only include character formatting. The style of individual characters within a paragraph can differ from the paragraph as a whole.

To apply a style, select the desired paragraph or character, then select the style from the Style drop-down menu on the Standard toolbar. The menu notes paragraph styles with a paragraph mark (¶) and character styles with an underlined letter *a*. Paragraph styles are applied to the paragraph that contains the insertion point or to multiple selected paragraphs. Character styles are applied to selected text.

If the current selection has a character style applied, the Style box on the Standard toolbar displays only the character style. Otherwise, you'll see the paragraph style. To see both the character and paragraph styles for a selection in Word 2002 or 2003, select Format → Reveal Formatting. In Word 97 or 2000, select Format → Style.

Character styles override paragraph styles. If you apply a paragraph style to an existing paragraph, it changes the format of all the characters in the paragraph, *except* the characters you manually formatted. For example, suppose you apply the Normal style to a paragraph and add special formatting to one word in the paragraph (say, you italicize the word and make it red for emphasis). If you later applied a new paragraph style, all the characters in the paragraph would change except for that one word.

NOTE

To quickly remove all character formatting, select a range of characters and press Ctrl-Spacebar. This causes the characters to revert to the character formatting defined in the paragraph style. To remove manual paragraph formatting from a paragraph, select the whole paragraph, including the paragraph mark, and press Ctrl-Q.

Shortcut Menus

If you have used Windows for any amount of time, you're probably familiar with shortcut menus—the contextual menus that pop up when you right-click an item. Right-clicking also works in Word and is a real time-saver. Generally, right-clicking an item inside the document window (text, graphics, etc.) provides access to the pertinent features that are available on Word's normal menus for grouping, ordering, and formatting that kind of object.

The following results when you right-click in the Word interface:

- When you right-click a selected word, paragraph, or just somewhere within text, you get a shortcut menu with editing commands (copy, cut, paste), formatting commands (font, paragraph, bullets, and numbering), some language tools, and a command for selecting all paragraphs in the document with the same style as the current paragraph.

- If you right-click text with special attributes (misspelled, indented, bulleted text, and so on), you get a shortcut menu with commands for dealing with that function (e.g., spelling corrections).

- If you right-click a table (or a selected part of a table), a shortcut menu provides you with most of the commands found on the Table menu.

- Right-click any command bar to display a list of common command bars you can toggle on or off.

- If you right-click the TRK button on the status bar, you can turn on Track Changes, highlight changes, and set other options.

- If you right-click the Spelling and Grammar Status button (the open book) on the status bar, you can hide spelling and grammar errors and set options.

Word lets you customize the commands on the shortcut menus—in fact, it is the only Office application aside from PowerPoint that lets you do so. First, select Tools → Customize, click the Toolbars tab, and check the Shortcut Menus box. This opens a special command bar named Shortcut Menus. The submenus below the three main menus (Text, Table, and Draw) correspond to all the shortcut menus available in Word. For example, select Text → Text to display the shortcut menu for basic text. To add a command to a menu, shortcut menu, or toolbar, click the Commands tab in the Customize dialog box and drag the command to the desired location. For example, you might want to add the ApplyHeading1, 2, and 3 commands to the Text shortcut menu to save yourself time.

NOTE

The Shortcut Menus command bar only stays open while the Customize dialog box is open. Its only purpose is to let you add commands to shortcut menus.

What Word Tries to Do for You

Word performs many behind-the-scenes actions that some people hate and some people love. You already learned about

AutoRecover, which saves files in the background every few minutes. Word offers three other big automated features: AutoCorrect, Smart Cut and Paste, and background spelling and grammar check.

AutoCorrect

When you type a list using asterisks as bullets, Word converts it to a bulleted list. When you accidentally type "teh", Word changes it to "the" as soon as you hit the spacebar. Word's AutoCorrect feature tries to fix these types of text and formatting problems.

NOTE

So, what if you like automatic corrections sometimes, but not all the time? Leave them enabled and then use the Undo command (Ctrl-Z) as soon as the correction is made. Undo should reverse the automatic correction and let you keep going. For instance, if you occasionally want a "straight quote," use Undo right after Word creates a smart curly quote.

You can also control what kind of corrections you want Word to apply. Select Tools → AutoCorrect to display the AutoCorrect dialog box. Two important tabs let you change the automatic options:

AutoCorrect
> This tab controls actual text corrections. The options at the top of the tab deal mostly with incorrect capitalization. The "Replace text as you type" option specifies whether Word should use the long list of corrections at the bottom of the tab. You can delete items from the list or add your own items by entering them in the topmost fields. In addition to the thousands of corrections built into Word, you can also create your own (covered in Part 2).

AutoFormat As You Type

The options on this tab control automatic formatting—bulleted and numbered lists, smart quotes (the curly quotes), and fraction characters, to name a few.

NOTE

In Word 97-2002, you can right-click any interface element and choose What's This? to see a description of its function. In Word 2003, press F1 to open a help window that documents the features on the dialog box.

Smart Cut and Paste

Smart Cut and Paste automatically controls how many spaces are placed before and after text when you paste it into a location. For the most part, this feature is benign. It is helpful to copy a group of words, paste them into a new paragraph, and have Word make one space at the beginning and end of the group. Depending on your tastes, you may want to fine-tune these settings.

First, select Tools → Options and click the Edit tab. You can check or uncheck the Use smart cut and paste box to turn the whole feature on or off.

In Word 2002 and 2003, you can fine-tune the Smart Cut and Paste option. Select Tools → Options, click the Edit tab, and then click the Settings button. Some of the more interesting options let you do the following:

- Set the options to the default used by Word 2002/2003 or by Word 97/2000
- Merge pasted lists with the surrounding list in the destination location
- Adjust table alignment when pasting tables or parts of tables into new locations
- Adjust sentence, word, and paragraph spacing when pasting

Spelling and Grammar

By default, Word checks both spelling and grammar in the background. Word puts squiggly red lines under words not found in its dictionary and squiggly green lines under suspected grammatical errors. Right-click the errors to see suggested corrections on the shortcut menu. While it sounds useful, most people find that having the errors marked in the document distracts them and slows down the display of longer documents. To remove the distractions, select Tools → Options, click the Spelling & Grammar tab, and choose one of the following:

- If you want Word to perform background checking, but not show the errors in the document, check the Hide spelling errors in this document box and the Hide grammatical errors in this document box.

- To turn background checking off altogether, uncheck the Check spelling as you type box and the Check grammar as you type box. Background checking degrades performance, especially in long documents. It's almost always more efficient to do a full spell and grammar check when you're done creating a document.

The rest of the options deal with *how* Word checks spelling and grammar (see Part 2).

The Most Common Word Complaints

You can't make everybody happy. Some people love the single document interface; some love the multiple document interface. Some like it when Word automatically formats bulleted and numbered lists; some don't. Fortunately, as you'll learn in this book, Word is pretty flexible.

Throughout this book, you'll find pointers on just about every option you can set and task you can perform in Word.

However, some options deserve special mention. Table 1 lists the top offenders—the features that annoy readers more than any others. The table describes the feature, lets you know whether it's on or off by default, and tells you how to change the setting.

Table 1. Most common Word complaints

Feature	Default	How to change
Word 2003 opens some documents in Reading Layout view.	Enabled	Select Tools → Options, click the General tab, and uncheck the Allow starting in Reading Layout box.
Word opens a separate window for each document.	Enabled	In Word 2002 and 2003, select Tools → Options, click the View tab, and uncheck the Windows in Taskbar box. You can't do anything about it in Word 2000.
Word does not show all of the commands on menus unless I click a down arrow.	Enabled	In Word 2002 and 2003, select Tools → Customize, click the Options tab, and check the Always show full menus box (uncheck the Menus show recently used commands first box in Word 2000.
There are red dashed underlines beneath names and dates, and annoying pop-ups appear when I move my pointer over them.	Enabled	Select Tools → Options, click the View tab, and uncheck the Smart tags box.
Word puts red and green squiggles under misspelled words and grammatical errors.	Enabled	Select Tools → Options, click the Spelling & Grammar tab, and check the Hide spelling errors in this document box, and the Hide grammatical errors in this document box.
Word automatically creates numbered and bulleted lists.	Enabled	Select Tools → AutoCorrect Options (Tools → AutoCorrect in Word 97 and 2000), click the AutoFormat As You Type tab, and uncheck the Automatic numbered lists box and the Automatic bulleted lists box.
Word inserts a drawing canvas whenever I create or insert a picture.	Enabled	Select Tools → Options, click the General tab, and uncheck the Automatically create drawing canvas when inserting AutoShapes box.

Table 1. Most common Word complaints (continued)

Feature	Default	How to change
When I type some words, Word pops up a balloon over the text.	Enabled	Select Tools → AutoCorrect Options (Tools → AutoCorrect in Word 97 and 2000), click the AutoText tab, and uncheck the Show AutoComplete Suggestions box (uncheck the Show AutoComplete tip for AutoText and dates box in Word 97 and 2000).
Word pops up balloons with reviewers' comments in them.	Enabled	Select Tools → Options, click the View tab, and uncheck the Screen Tips box.
Word pops up balloons with button names whenever I point at toolbar buttons.	Enabled	Select Tools → Customize, click the Options tab, and uncheck the Show ScreenTips on toolbars box.
Word keeps asking me if I want to update a style whenever I format text.	Disabled	In Word 2002 and 2003, select Tools → Options, click the Edit tab, and uncheck the Prompt to update style box.
Word shows empty boxes with an "x" in them instead of pictures.	Disabled	Select Tools → Options, click the View tab, and uncheck the Picture placeholders box.
Word stores personal information about me in my documents.	Enabled	In Word 2002 and 2003, select Tools → Options, click the Security tab, and check the Remove personal information from file properties on save box (check the Remove personal information from this file on save box in Word 2002).

PART II

Word Tasks

This section of the book gives you quick answers about how to perform common and not-so-common (but very useful) tasks in Word. The tasks are divided into the following sixteen categories:

- Working with Files
- Printing
- Moving Around in a Document
- Entering and Editing Text
- Formatting
- Changing Your View
- Controlling the Flow of a Document
- Inserting Fields and Reference Items
- Inserting Objects
- Working with Tables
- Spelling and Other Tools
- Setting Other Word Options
- Getting Help
- Customizing Word
- Collaborating
- Using Macros

Within these categories, you will find concise instructions for completing the task. For some tasks, you will see multiple solutions.

Working with Files

Follow these steps to create, find, save, and otherwise work with files.

Open a document

Select File → Open, press Ctrl-O, or click the Open button to display the Open dialog box and browse for an existing document. Use the Open button's drop-down list to open a document in different ways (read-only, open a copy, open and repair, etc.).

Create a new Word document without starting Word

Right-click any blank space in a folder or desktop and select New → Microsoft Word Document.

Create a new document within Word

Click the New Blank Document button on the Standard toolbar or press Ctrl-N to create a new blank document based on the *Normal.dot* template.

Select File → New to create a blank document of any type using the New Document task pane (Word 2002 and 2003) or the New Document dialog box (Word 97 and 2000).

Create a document from a template

In Word 2003, select File → New and click the On my computer link (or click one of the other links) in the New Document task pane.

In Word 2002, select File → New and click the General Templates link in the New Document task pane.

In Word 97 and 2000, select File → New, click a tab (Legal Pleadings, Letters and Faxes, Memos, etc), and choose a template.

Find a Document

In Word 2003, select File → File Search (File → Search in Word 2002) and enter the text, location, and file types you want to search. Click the Advanced Search link to search using multiple criteria in one step.

In Word 97 and 2000, use File → Open, and select Find from the Tools menu.

Save a document

Select File → Save, click the Save button, or press Ctrl-S to save your work on a document.

Select File → Save As to save using a different name or in a different location. Selecting File → Save opens the Save As dialog box the first time you save a document.

Select File → Save as Web Page (Save as HTML in Word 97) to convert a document to HTML.

Close all open documents with one command

Hold down the Shift key while opening the File menu to change the Close command to Close All.

To add a Close All button to a toolbar or menu, select Tools → Customize → Commands. Select the File command category and then drag the Close All command to the desired location. See "Customizing Word" later in this part.

Keep track of different versions of documents

Select File → Versions, and click the Save Now button to save recent work as a new version and enter comments. Saved versions are listed by date and time.

Change the summary information for a document

Select File → Properties, click the Summary tab and enter information about the document.

> ### Add my own templates to the Templates dialog box
>
> In Word 2000-2003, save your template in *C:\Documents and Settings\<username>\Application Data\ Microsoft\Templates* (for Windows 2000/XP) or in *C:\Windows\Application Data\Microsoft\Templates* (for Windows 9x/Me).
>
> In Word 97, save your template in *C:\Program Files\ Microsoft Office\Templates* (for any Windows version). Create a new subfolder in the Templates folder to create a new tab on the Templates dialog.

Save a preview picture with a template

Select File → Properties, click the Summary tab and check the Save preview picture box. Windows displays a preview picture showing the first page of the document for use when viewing thumbnails.

Set up custom properties for a document

Select File → Properties, click the Custom tab, select the properties you want to add from the list, and click the Add button.

Change how many recently used files are shown on the File menu

Select Tools → Options, click the General tab, turn the Recently used file list option on or off, and select from 1– 9 recent files to appear.

Copy a backup of the previous version of a document whenever I save

Select Tools → Options, click the Save tab, and check the Always create backup copy box. Word copies the previous version and creates a new file in the same folder with a *.wbk* extension.

Change the default format used to save documents

Select Tools → Options, click the Save tab, and choose a format from the Save Word files as drop-down menu.

> **Make sure others have the fonts used in my document**
>
> Select Tools → Options, click the Save tab, and check the Embed TrueType fonts box. You can also embed only the characters in use (and with Word 2000-2003, skip the common system fonts), since font embedding increases file size..

02+ *Choose whether Smart Tags are saved in my document*

Select Tools → Options, click the Save tab, and check the Embed smart tags box. There's also an option that lets you Save smart tags as XML properties in web pages.

Control the default locations where files and templates are saved

Select Tools → Options, click the File Locations tab, choose a file type, and click the Modify button. See Part 3 for a list of default file locations.

02+ *Keep personal information from being saved with a document*

Select Tools → Options, click the Security tab, and check the Remove personal information from file properties on save box (check the Remove personal information from this file on save box in Word 2002).

02+ *Recover a document after Word crashes*

When you start Word, the Document Recovery task pane opens automatically and lists all recovered files. You can compare the recovered files to the previously saved versions and decide which to keep.

Change how often AutoRecover information is saved

Select Tools → Options, click the Save tab, turn the Save AutoRecover info every *xx* minutes option on or off, and enter a value for the number of minutes.

Change where AutoRecover information is saved

Select Tools → Options, click the File Locations tab, select AutoRecover files from the list of file types, and click the Modify button.

> **Recover the text without formatting from any document**
>
> Select Tools → Options, click the General tab, and check the Confirm conversion at Open box. Next, select File → Open, find the file, and choose Recover Text from Any File from the Files of type drop-down menu.

`02+` *Recover Word when the program hangs*

Select Start → All Programs → Microsoft Office Tools → Microsoft Office Application Recovery. This dialog box lets you end a frozen program (losing all document changes) or attempt to recover the program and any documents.

`02+` *Start Word in safe mode when it won't start normally*

Hold down the Ctrl key when you start Word or type word.exe /safe at the command prompt or in the Start → Run dialog. Safe mode is normally used for troubleshooting startup problems or opening documents that have problem-causing macros or add-ins. Several restrictions apply in safe mode. Templates cannot be saved, the Office Assistant is not loaded, customizations are not loaded, recovered documents are not opened, preferences cannot be saved, and custom AutoCorrect lists are not loaded (though the default AutoCorrect entries continue to work).

`02+` *Enable items that are disabled in safe mode*

Select Help → About Microsoft Word and click the Disabled Items button. Next, select the items you want to enable and click the Enable button.

`03+` *Set restricted permissions on a document*

Select File → Permission → Do Not Distribute or File → Permission → Restrict Permission As. Set the users or groups that should have access to the document, the level of access they should have (view the content, change the content, and when the content expires), and click the OK button.

NOTE

Using restricted permissions comes with a number of ca-
veats. First, it is only available in Office 2003 Professional Edition. Second, in order to use the Information Rights
Management technology that allows content restriction,
you must either have an IRM server set up on your local
network (which requires Windows Server 2003) or use
the Microsoft .NET Passport service (which lets you
widely distribute protected documents). People you send
the document to must have access to the same service you
use to protect the content. Third, once you restrict content, the restrictions become part of the document and
you must be able to access the selected IRM server to
view the document. If you can't, you may find yourself
locked out of your own documents.

Printing

The following tasks show you various ways to print, how to
set up a page and control printer options, and how to use the
Print Preview feature.

Print a document
> Select File → Print or press Ctrl-P. Next, select your
> printer, any options, and click the Print button.

Print a document from Windows
> Right-click the document (or group of selected docu-
> ments) and select Print from the shortcut menu. Word
> opens long enough to print the document using default
> settings and then closes.

Print one copy of a document without using the Print dialog box
> Click the Print button on the Standard toolbar to print
> one copy of the document using default settings.

Print to a file instead of a printer
> Select File → Print, check the Print to file box, click the
> OK button, then supply a filename and destination.

Print using draft output to save time and ink

Select File → Print, click the Options button, and check the Draft output box.

You can also select Tools → Options, click the Print tab, and check the Draft output box.

Choose what information is printed along with a document

Select File → Print, click the Options button (or select Tools → Options and click the Print tab), and select the desired options in the Include with document section of the dialog box.

Set other printing options

Select File → Print, click the Options button (or select Tools → Options and click the Print tab), and make your changes.

Change the margins for a section or an entire document

Select File → Page Setup, click the Margins tab, and use the boxes in the Margins section of the dialog box. A gutter is the inside space between two facing pages, usually used for binding a book.

Change page orientation for a section or document

In Word 2002 and 2003, select File → Page Setup, click the Margins tab, and choose Portrait or Landscape.

In Word 97 and 2000, select File → Page Setup, click the Paper Size tab, and choose Portrait or Landscape.

`00+` *Change how multiple pages are printed*

Select File → Print and choose up to sixteen pages on one sheet of paper from the Pages per sheet drop-down menu.

In Word 2002 and 2003, you can also select File → Page Setup, click the Margins tab, and select an option from the Multiple pages drop-down menu. The mirror margins option creates facing-page layouts (where left and right pages face one another), 2 pages per sheet prints two identical pages on each sheet of paper, and Book fold puts two different pages on a single sheet. This last option is designed for documents (like invitations) that fold in the middle. In Word 97 and 2000, the Margins tab offers only two options: Mirror margins and 2 pages per sheet.

Configure settings for paper size, type, and source

In Word 2002 and 2003, select File → Page Setup and click the Paper tab. Word 97 and 2000 have separate Paper Size and Paper Source tabs.

Change how headers and footers are printed

Select File → Page Setup, click the Layout tab, and use the options in the Headers and Footers section of the dialog box. In Word 97 and 2000, the header and footer distance settings are on the Margins tab.

Change the vertical alignment of pages in a section or document

Select File → Page Setup, click the Layout tab, and select an option from the Vertical alignment drop-down menu.

Print pages in reverse order (last to first)

Select File → Print, click the Options button (or select Tools → Options and click the Print tab), and check the Reverse print order box.

02+ *Print two-sided pages without add-on software*

If you have a duplex printer (one that can print both sides of paper at once), select File → Print, click the Options button (or select Tools → Options and click the Print tab), and use the check boxes (Front of the sheet and Back of the sheet) at the bottom of the dialog box.

If you don't have a duplex printer, select File → Print and check the Manual duplex box. After one side prints, Word prompts you to reinsert the paper to print on the other side.

NOTE

In Word 97 or 2000, you can approximate the Manual duplex option by printing first all odd pages in reverse order, flipping the pages over, and then printing all even pages.

Print a folded booklet

To create a folded booklet, start with a blank document. Select File → Page Setup, click the Margins tab, and change the Multiple pages selection to Book fold. Once you create and format your booklet, select File → Print and make sure you're set up to print two-sided pages (see the previous task).

If you have an existing document, your best bet is to create a new blank document, set it up as a folded booklet, and then copy and paste the text from your original document into the new document.

Print additional non-text information in a document

Select File → Print and select an option such as document properties, markup, styles, AutoText entries, or shortcut keys from the Print what drop-down menu. The exact list of options depends on your version of Word.

Preview a document before printing

Select File → Print Preview. You can zoom and view multiple pages at once. Make sure you use the Close button on the toolbar to return to the regular document view. You can also just press the Esc key.

Moving Around in a Document

This section shows you how to find and replace text, browse for specific objects, move the insertion point, and change the display view of a document.

Scroll around in a document

Click the single arrows in the vertical scroll bar to move up and down one line at a time. Click the double arrows to move up or down one page. Drag the scroll handle to move the view freely; a pop-up balloon shows the page and major headings as you scroll past. Scrolling using the scroll bars changes your view, but does *not* move the insertion point. Use the horizontal scroll bar much as you would the vertical scroll bar.

Hide the scroll bars

Select Tools → Options, click the View tab, and use the Horizontal and Vertical scroll bar options.

Move the insertion point using the keyboard

Use the Left and Right arrows to move one character at a time. Press Ctrl and an arrow key to move one word at a time. Press Shift-Ctrl-arrow key to select text while the cursor moves.

Use the Up and down arrows to move one line at a time. Press Ctrl and an arrow key to move one paragraph at a time. Press Shift-Shift-arrow key to select text while moving.

See a complete list of movement keys in Part 3.

See where the screen view is in the document

The left-most number on the status bar (Page *x*) displays the number of the page you are viewing (see Figure 3). You can also click and hold the vertical scroll handle to see the page and nearest heading (see Figure 8).

Figure 8. View page numbers with the vertical scroll bar

See where the insertion point is in the document

The second and third values on the status bar (Sec *x* and *y/yy*) show the section and page where the insertion point is located. "At" shows distance from the top margin of the current page, "Ln" shows the line number, and "Col" shows the column number.

03+ *Center the view on the insertion point*

Click any movement key (such as the right arrow) to center the view (i.e., make the display show where the insertion point is). This presumes you have disabled Smart cursoring. (Select Tools → Options, click the Edit tab, and uncheck the Use smart cursoring box.) If Smart Cursoring is enabled, moving the cursor by clicking an arrow key actually brings the cursor to your current location instead of bringing your current location to the cursor.

Go to a specific location in a document

Select Edit → Go To or press Ctrl-G, select the object (page, table, graphic, etc.), and click the Previous or Next button to jump to objects of that type. Enter a specific value (e.g., page number, bookmark name) to go directly to it.

Find specific text in a document

Select Edit → Find or press Ctrl-F, enter your search text, and click the Find Next button.

Return to where I left off the last time I had the document open

Press Shift-F5 when you first open the document. If the document is already open, Shift-F5 lets you rotate between the last three places you made changes.

02+ *Find and select all occurrences of specific text in a document*

Select Edit → Find, enter your search text, check the Highlight all items found in box, and click the Find All button. Word selects all occurrences in the document. Select Edit → Copy to copy all occurrences to the clipboard.

> ### *Find specific formatting in a document*
> Select Edit → Find and click the More button to reveal additional search options. Next, click the Format button and make a selection from the drop-down menu. In the dialog box, specify any formatting criteria you want to search for (such as bold). Each selection adds a format to the search criteria. Click the No Formatting button to remove all formatting from the search.

Find special characters in a document
Select Edit → Find and click the More button to reveal additional search options. Next, click the Special button and make a selection from the drop-down menu. See Part 3 for a list of search codes you can type directly into the Find and Replace dialog box.

Find and replace text in a document
Select Edit → Replace or press Ctrl-H and enter the desired text into the find and replace fields. Click the Find Next button to select the next occurrence in the document. Click the Replace button to replace the current selection or Replace All to replace all found occurrences.

Find and replace specific formatting
Select Edit → Replace and click the More button to reveal additional search options. Next, click the Format button and make a selection from the drop-down menu.

Find and replace special characters
Select Edit → Replace and click the More button to reveal additional search options. Next, click the Special button and make a selection from the drop-down menu.

Find or replace noun or adjective forms or verb tenses
Select Edit → Find or Edit → Replace. Click the More button to reveal additional search options and check the Find all word forms box.

Browse a document by specific objects

Click the Select Browse Object button (at the bottom of the vertical scroll bar) or press Ctrl-Alt-Home and select the type of object to browse from the pop-up menu. Click the Previous and Next buttons (or Ctrl-Page Up and Ctrl-Page Down) to do the browsing.

TIP

There is no way to assign a custom keyboard shortcut directly to the Find Next command (although Alt-F works with the dialog box open). If you want to close the Find dialog box and still do a Find Next, perform the first search using the dialog box, close the dialog box, and then use Ctrl-Page Down or Shift-F4 to find subsequent occurrences.

Entering and Editing Text

This section will show you how to insert text, symbols, and special characters; select characters, words, and paragraphs; and copy and paste text. This section also covers methods of automatic text entry, including AutoCorrect and AutoText. As you learned in Part 1, AutoCorrect fixes common text and formatting problems automatically. For example, it can turn asterisks into bullets, change "teh" to "the", and automatically apply other types of formatting. Some people also use AutoCorrect to insert boilerplate text (for example, you could type "addr" to insert an address), although AutoText works much better. AutoText lets you store frequently used text (with formatting) and graphics to quickly insert in your document.

Using AutoText and AutoCorrect

Create an AutoText entry for inserting frequently used text and graphics

In the document window, select the text or graphic you want to use. Select Insert → AutoText → AutoText and

---

click the Add button to create the entry. If you want, enter a different name for the entry before you click the Add button.

Insert an AutoText entry

Select Insert → AutoText and select an AutoText entry from one of the submenus. You can also type the first few letters of the entry directly into the document and press the F3 key. If you enable Screen Tips (select Tools → Options, click the View tab, and check the Screen Tips box), a pop-up balloon with the AutoText entry also appears after you type the first few letters. Press the Enter key to accept the suggestion and insert the AutoText.

TIP

Right-click anywhere on the toolbar area and select Auto-Text to show a toolbar with all the AutoText entries.

Turn off the pop-up AutoComplete suggestions for AutoText entries

Select Tools → Options, click the View tab, and uncheck the Screen Tips box. This also turns off all other screen tips, including those that appear when the pointer passes over toolbar buttons.

Change an AutoText entry

Create a new AutoText entry and give it the same name as the AutoText entry you want to replace. Or select Insert → AutoText → AutoText, select the entry, and click the Delete button. Type a new entry in the "Enter AutoText entries here" field and click the Add button.

Print a reference list of all AutoText entries

Select File → Print and from the Print what drop-down menu, select AutoText entries and click the OK button.

Undo an AutoCorrect insertion

Word inserts AutoCorrect entries (like replacing "(c)" with the copyright symbol) automatically as you type. As soon as it happens, choose Edit → Undo or press Ctrl-Z to undo the autocorrection.

Control AutoCorrect options
Select Tools → AutoCorrect Options (Tools → AutoCorrect in Word 97 and 2000) and click the AutoCorrect tab.

Inserting Text and Other Elements

Insert the current date and time into a document
Select Insert → Date and Time and select the Update automatically option to always display the current date and time in the document.

Insert a symbol
Select Insert → Symbol and click the Symbols tab. Choose a font and subset, select the symbol, and click the Insert button. For frequently used symbols, click the Shortcut Key button to assign a keyboard shortcut. For a list of built-in shortcut keys for common symbols, see Part 3.

Insert a special character
Select Insert → Symbol and click the Special Characters tab. Choose a special character from the list and click the Insert button.

Keep text from disappearing as you type

If new characters that you type replace existing characters (instead of just bumping them to the right to make room for the new text), the Overtype feature is turned on. (You'll see OVR light up in the status bar.) To turn it off, press the Insert key or double-click the word OVR on the status bar. You can also select Tools → Options, click the Edit tab, and uncheck the Overtype mode box.

Selecting Text

Select a character

Click and drag over the character. To select the character immediately left or right of the insertion point, hold down the Shift key and press the left or right arrow key. Keep pressing the arrow key to extend the selection one character at a time in that direction.

Select a word

Double-click the word. Press Ctrl-Shift-Left (or Right) to select the word immediately to the left or right. Keep pressing the arrow keys to extend the selection one word at a time.

Select a sentence

Click and drag over the sentence.

TIP

The SentLeftExtend and SentRightExtend commands extend the selection one sentence to the left or right (much like Shift-Left [or Right] extends by characters). See the "Customizing Word" section for instructions on putting them on a toolbar or assigning shortcut keys.

Select a paragraph

Triple-click the paragraph or double click in the left margin. Press Ctrl-Shift-Up (or Down) to extend a selection from the insertion point to the beginning or end of the paragraph. Keep pressing the up or down arrow to extend the selection one paragraph at a time.

Select a single line of text

Press Shift-End to select all text from the insertion point to the right end of the current line. Press Shift-Home to select all text from the insertion point to the left end of the current line.

Select a specific group of characters

Click one location and then Shift-click another location to select all full words between the two locations.

<u>02+</u> *Select multiple, non-contiguous pieces of text*

> Make the first selection using any method (e.g., double-click to select a word). Hold down the Ctrl key and make another selection elsewhere in the document.

<u>02+</u>
> **Select all paragraphs using a particular style or format**
>
> Make a selection or place the insertion point in the appropriate location, then choose Format → Styles and Formatting and click the Select All button.
>
> You can also right-click a selection or location and choose Select Text with Similar Formatting from the shortcut menu.

<u>02+</u> *Change whether the paragraph mark is selected along with a paragraph*

> Select Tools → Options, click the Edit tab, and check the Use smart paragraph selection box. If you select the paragraph mark, the formatting moves with the paragraph. This option applies only when you drag to select the paragraph. If you triple-click the paragraph, you always select the paragraph mark.

Change whether whole words are automatically selected when you drag over them

> Select Tools → Options, click the Edit tab, and check or uncheck the When selecting, automatically select entire word box.

Use the Extend Selection (EXT) feature

> Press the F8 key or double-click EXT on the status bar to enter the Extend Selection mode. In this mode, take one of the following actions:
>
> - Click anywhere to extend the selection from the insertion point.
> - Use the arrow keys to extend the selection one line (up and down arrows) or one character (left and right arrows) at a time.

- Press the F8 key repeatedly to extend the selection. The first time you press the F8 key after entering EXT mode, it selects the word closest to the insertion point. The second time it selects the entire sentence, the third time the entire paragraph, and the fourth time the whole document.

- Press Esc to exit EXT mode.

Copying and Pasting

Move or copy text by dragging

Select the text using any method and then click and drag the text to a new location. You can drag somewhere else in the same document, to another open document, or to open a document in another program that supports it (such as Excel or Outlook). To copy text, hold down the Ctrl key while you click and drag.

TIP

Drag a selection to the Windows Desktop to create a *document scrap*—a special file with an *.shs* extension. You can open this file directly, but you can also drag it into any open document to insert the text with its original formatting.

02+ *Get rid of the paste options button that appears over text when you paste*

Select Tools → Options, click the Edit tab, and uncheck the Show Paste Options buttons box.

02+ *Copy multiple items to the Office Clipboard*

The Office Clipboard lets you collect (by copying or cutting) up to 24 items from any Office document (12 items in Word 2000). Select Edit → Office Clipboard and copy items using standard copy and cut commands.

Click the Paste All button to paste items to the current location. Click the Clear All button to clear the clipboard.

Change whether the Office Clipboard appears when you copy multiple items

    Select Edit → Office Clipboard and click the Options button. The Show Office Clipboard Automatically option forces the clipboard to appear when you copy two items consecutively. The Collect Without Showing Office Clipboard option lets you collect items without the task pane showing.

Paste items using alternate or special formatting

    Select Edit → Paste Special, choose a format, and click the OK button.

Formatting

This section shows you how to apply character and paragraph formatting, use and organize formatting styles, create bulleted and numbered lists, and add borders and background colors.

Character Formatting

Apply basic font formatting

    Select Format → Font and click the Font tab. Set the font, style, size, and color for the selected text, or for new text typed at the insertion point. You can also access these controls on the Formatting toolbar or by right-clicking and selecting Font.

Apply special font effects

    Select Format → Font, click the Font tab, and use any of the options in the Effects section.

Hide text

Select the text you want to hide, then select Format → Font, click the Font tab, and check the Hidden box. To see hidden text, use the Show/Hide button on the Standard toolbar or select Tools → Options, click the View tab, and check the Hidden text box.

Use a drop cap

Select Format → Drop Cap. You can place a drop cap at the beginning of a line or within the text. You can also select a font for the capitalized letter, specify how many lines to drop (1–3), and dictate its distance from surrounding text.

Set a default font

Select Format → Font, click the Font tab, select the font and its attributes, and then click the Default button. Word saves the changes in *Normal.dot*.

Change the spacing between characters

Select Format → Font and click the Character Spacing tab. Scale stretches or condenses text horizontally. Options in the Spacing menu increase or reduce the space between characters. Position changes the position of the text vertically in relation to the baseline. Kerning changes the spacing between certain predefined letter combinations so that words look more evenly spaced; you can specify at which font size kerning occurs.

Change the case of a selection

Select Format → Change Case and choose a case type. Or press Shift-F3 to cycle through case types (all caps, all lower case, leading cap).

TIP

Select Tools → AutoCorrect Options (Tools → AutoCorrect in Word 97 and 2000) and click the AutoCorrect tab to modify whether Word automatically applies corrections to capitalization errors, typos, and spelling errors.

Use or remove text animations

Select Format → Font and click the Text Effects tab (In Word 97, click the Animation tab).

Turn text animations on or off without removing them from a document

Select Tools → Options, click the View tab, and use the Animated text box.

Paragraph Formatting

Change the alignment of a paragraph

Place the insertion point in a paragraph or select one or more paragraphs. Then click the Align Left, Center, Align Right, and Justify buttons on the Formatting toolbar or select Format → Paragraph, click the Indents and Spacing tab, and choose an alignment.

Change the indentation of a paragraph

Place the insertion point at the beginning of a paragraph or select multiple paragraphs, then take one of the following actions:

- Set the left indent by dragging the Left Indent marker (the rectangular one—see Figure 9) on the horizontal ruler or select Format → Paragraph, click the Indents and Spacing tab, and enter a Left indent value.

- Set the first line indent by pressing Tab to move the text over one tab stop or dragging the First Line Indent marker on the horizontal ruler to the desired location. You can also select Format → Paragraph, click the Indents and Spacing tab, choose First line from the Special drop-down menu, and enter an exact measurement.

- Set the right indent by dragging the Right Indent marker on the ruler or set exact measurements on the Indents and Spacing tab as described above.

- Set the hanging indent (which controls all but the first line) by dragging the Hanging Indent marker or select Format → Paragraph, click the Indents and

Spacing tab, and choose Hanging from the Special drop-down menu.

Change the line spacing between and within paragraphs

Select the paragraph (or just place the insertion point in it) and select Format → Paragraph and click the Indents and Spacing tab. Use the Before option to set the blank space before a paragraph, the After option to set the space following the paragraph, and the Line spacing option to set the distance between lines within the paragraph.

Set tab stops

Click the tab selector button at the far left in the ruler to cycle through the available tab types, and then click the ruler to place stops.

Select Format → Tabs to show exact locations of existing tab stops. Type a new location in the Tab stop position box (in the default measurement unit), choose an alignment for the type of tab stop, and click the Set button to create a new tab stop.

To change a tab stop, select Format → Tabs and select a tab stop. Change any options and click the Set button to modify the stop. Click the Clear button to remove a tab stop or the Clear All button to remove all customized stops.

Change the default spacing between tab stops

Select Format → Tabs and enter a Default tab stops value.

Set up a leader (such as dashed lines) between tab stops

Select Format → Tabs and choose a Leader. Leaders serve to connect text. A common example is the row of dots you often see connecting an entry in a table of contents and the page number for that entry.

Show line numbers in a document

Line numbers are displayed only in Print Layout view (Page Layout view in Word 97). To show line numbers:

1. Select View → Print Layout.

2. Select File → Page Setup, click the Layout tab, and click the Line Numbers button.

3. Check the Add line numbering box and set numbering options.

Skip line numbering for specific paragraphs

Select the paragraphs, then select Format → Paragraph, click the Line and Page Breaks tab, and check the Suppress line numbers box.

Working with Formats and Styles

Determine the formats used on a paragraph or character

In Word 2002 and 2003, select the paragraph or characters, then select Format → Reveal Formatting. The Reveal Formatting pane shows you the font, paragraph, and section formatting applied to the selection.

In Word 97 and 2000 (as well as 2002), select Help → What's This? or press Shift-F1 and the pointer turns into a question mark. Click the text for a pop-up description of the formatting.

NOTE

The What's This? feature is not available in Word 2003.

02+ *Select all the text in a document with the same formatting*

Make a selection or place the insertion point in the appropriate location, select Format → Styles and Formatting, and click the Select All button.

You can also right-click a selection or location and choose Select Text with Similar Formatting from the shortcut menu.

> **Remove formatting or styles from selected text**
>
> Select the text and press Ctrl-Spacebar.
>
> In Word 2002 and 2003, you can also select the text and then choose Clear Formatting from the Style drop-down menu.

Copy formatting to another selection

Select the text or paragraph with the formatting you want to copy. Click the Format Painter button (it looks like a little paintbrush) on the Standard toolbar. Drag the pointer over the selection to which you want to copy the formatting.

TIP

Double-click the Format Painter button to "paint" formatting on multiple selections. Click the button again to release it.

Apply consistent sets of formatting using a character style

Character styles are collections of formats that affect characters within a paragraph and override formatting at the paragraph level. Apply a character style using the Style drop-down menu. Character styles have an underlined "a" next to them in the drop-down Style menu and the Style dialog box.

Apply consistent sets of formatting using a paragraph style

Paragraph styles affect the formatting of entire paragraphs, and can hold the same kinds of formatting as a character style and more. Apply a paragraph style using the Style drop-down menu. Paragraph styles have a paragraph mark next to them in the drop-down Style menu and in the Style dialog box.

Modify a style

In Word 2002 and 2003, select Format → Styles and Formatting, click the down arrow next to the style you want to change (or right-click the style), and choose Modify.

In the dialog box, you can change the name, style type, font, font size, and other elements. Check the Add to template box to add the style to the template attached to the document. Check the Automatically update box to update the style when you apply manual formatting to any paragraph with the style.

In Word 97 and 2000, select Format → Style, choose a style from the list, and click the Modify button.

NOTE

When you modify a style, you also modify the formatting of every paragraph or character in the document to which that style is applied.

Rename a style

Select Tools → Templates and Add-Ins, click the Organizer button, and click the Styles tab. In the list on the left, select the style and click the Rename button.

Create a new style

In Word 2002 and 2003, select Format → Styles and Formatting and click the New Style button. The selections shown in the New Style dialog box are based on the paragraph that contained the insertion point (or the characters that were selected for character styles).

In Word 97 and 2000, select Format → Style and click the New button.

Delete a style

In Word 2002 and 2003, select Format → Styles and Formatting, click the down arrow next to a style, and choose Delete. In Word 97 and 2000, select Format → Style, choose a style, and click the Delete button. If you delete a style that you created, Word applies the Normal style to all paragraphs using that style.

In all versions, you can also select Tools → Templates and Add- Ins, click the Organizer button, click the Styles

---

tab, select one or more styles from the list on the left, and click the Delete button.

Always have one paragraph style follow another

In Word 2002 and 2003, select Format → Styles and Formatting, click the down arrow next to a style and choose Modify. Select a style from the Style for following paragraph drop-down menu.

In Word 97 and 2000, select Format → Style, click the Modify button, and select a style from the Style for following paragraph drop-down menu.

Automatically update a style when you apply manual formatting to a paragraph using that style

In Word 2002 and 2003, select Format → Styles and Formatting, click the down arrow next a style and choose Modify. Check the Automatically update box.

In Word 97 and 2000, select Format → Style, click the Modify button, and check Automatically update box.

Preview styles used in a template

Select Format → Theme and click the Style Gallery button (Format → Style Gallery in Word 97). Select a template to show what the current document will look like with styles from that template. Select the Example option to see the styles in a sample document. Select the Style samples option to see an example of each style in the template. If you click the OK button, Word copies all styles from the template to the current document.

Copy styles between documents or templates

Select Tools → Templates and Add-Ins, click the Organizer button, and click the Styles tab. Open the two Styles available in drop-down menus (see Figure 9) to choose the two documents (or templates) whose styles you want to manage. Styles are listed above. Select one or more styles in one document and click the Copy button to copy them to the other open document.

TIP

You can manage AutoText entries, toolbars, and macros in the same way as styles, using the other tabs on the Organizer dialog box.

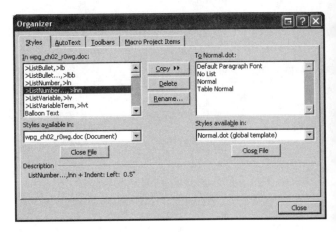

Figure 9. Organizing styles

Show style names to the left of a document

Select Tools → Options, click the View tab, and set the Style area width value to anything other than zero.

`02+` *Have Word track formatting changes in a document*

Select Tools → Options, click the Edit tab, and check the Keep track of formatting box. Formatting changes are shown along with tracked changes. See the "Collaborating" section later in this part.

Have Word show formatting marks

Select Tools → Options, click the View tab, and select options from the Formatting marks section (Nonprinting characters section in Word 97). Selecting the All option is the same as using the Show/Hide button on the Standard toolbar. Even when the Show/Hide button is not turned on, individually selected format options are shown in the document.

02+ *Have Word mark inconsistencies in formatting*

Select Tools → Options, click the Edit tab, and check the Mark formatting inconsistencies box. Word marks inconsistent formatting (such as some headings using bold and others not) with squiggly blue underlines. Right-click an inconsistency for suggestions.

Have Word format a document automatically

Select Format → AutoFormat. Choose the AutoFormat now option to format the document all at once using current AutoFormat options. Choose the AutoFormat and review each change option to accept or reject each change.

Change the options Word uses for AutoFormat

Select Format → AutoFormat, click the Options button, and click the AutoFormat tab. You can also select Tools → AutoCorrect Options (Tools → AutoCorrect in Word 97 and 2000), and click the AutoFormat tab.

Change the options Word uses to automatically format while you type

Select Tools → AutoCorrect Options (Tools → AutoCorrect in Word 97 and 2000) and click the AutoFormat As You Type tab.

0+ *Use Click and Type to automatically format text and graphics*

Select View → Print Layout or View → Web Layout. Click somewhere in a blank area of the document where you want to enter text. The pointer changes shape as you move it to show you how the text will be formatted (see

Figure 10). When the pointer indicates the kind of text you want to enter, double-click and start typing.

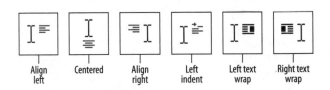

Figure 10. Click and Type options

00+ *Change the default paragraph style used by Click and Type*
Select Tools → Options, click the Edit tab, and choose a style from Default paragraph style drop-down menu.

00+ *Disable Click and Type*
Select Tools → Options, click the Edit tab, and uncheck the Enable click and type box.

Creating Lists

Create a basic bulleted or numbered list
Type a bullet symbol (asterisk or hyphen or number), followed by a space, followed by text. Press Enter and Word formats the list automatically.

You can also click the Numbering or Bullets button on the Formatting toolbar.

Create a list with a different bulleting or numbering style
Select Format → Bullets and Numbering, select the Bulleted, Numbered, or Outline Numbered tab depending on your need, select the type of bullet or number to use, and click the OK button.

Use a picture, character, or symbol as a bullet
Select Format → Bullets and Numbering, click the Bulleted tab, choose a bullet style, and click the Customize button. Next, click the Font button to change font prop-

erties or the Character button (Bullet button in Word 97 and 2000) to use a symbol or character. In Word 2000-2003, click the Picture button to use a clip art bullet.

Change the positioning of bullets and bulleted text
Select Format → Bullets and Numbering, click the Bulleted tab, and click the Customize button. Change the values in the Bullet position and Text position sections.

Change the indentation of one or more lines in a list
Select the lines and press Tab or Shift-Tab. Or select the lines and click the Decrease Indent or Increase Indent button on the Formatting toolbar.

Reset a list to use the default bulleting or numbering style
Select Format → Bullets and Numbering and click the Reset button.

TIP

Right-click an existing list and choose Bullets and Numbering for quicker access.

Restart the numbering on a list instead of continuing numbering from the previous list
Select Format → Bullets and Numbering, click the Numbered tab, and choose the Restart numbering option.

In Word 2002 and 2003, right-click the first line in the list and choose Restart numbering.

Continue the numbering from a previous list
Select Format → Bullets and Numbering, click the Numbered tab, and choose the Continue previous list option.

In Word 2002 and 2003, right-click the first line in the list and choose Continue Numbering.

Start a numbered list using a particular number
Select Format → Bullets and Numbering, click the Numbered tab, click the Customize button, and enter a Start at value.

Adjust the number style and position in a numbered list
> Select Format → Bullets and Numbering, click the Numbered tab, and click the Customize button.

Turn off automatic bulleting and numbering
> Select Tools → AutoCorrect Options (Tools → AutoCorrect in Word 97 and 2000), click the AutoFormat As You Type tab, and uncheck the Automatic bulleted lists box and the Automatic numbered lists box.

Combine multiple lists into a single list
> In Word 2002 and 2003, select a list, choose Edit → Copy or Edit → Cut, place the insertion point in the line below the list you want to add to, and then choose Edit → Paste. Word automatically renumbers the list for you.
>
> In Word 97 and 2000, you can still paste a list into another list, but Word does not automatically renumber it. Select the entire list and then click the Numbering button on the Formatting toolbar to renumber the list.

Working with Borders and Background Colors

Apply or change a border for a paragraph, selected text, or a table
> Select Format → Borders and Shading and click the Borders tab. Choose a type of border, a line style, and color. Click the buttons around the preview to turn on or off individual borders. Click the OK button to apply the border.

Apply or change page borders for all pages in a document or section
> Select Format → Borders and Shading and click the Page Border tab. This works the same as paragraph or table borders, but applies borders to all pages in a section or the whole document.

Shade a paragraph or selected text with a color or pattern
Select Format → Borders and Shading and click the Shading tab. Select a fill color or pattern, and choose whether to apply it to the border encircling a paragraph, table element, or the actual text within.

Set a background color for a document used as a web page
Select Format → Background and select a color from the palette or choose More Colors.

2+ *Set a background watermark for a printed document*
Select Format → Background → Printed Watermark.

0+ *Set a theme for a document*
Select Format → Theme. Select a theme from the list to see an example of what it looks like. Click the OK button to copy all styles to the current document. Note: this may change Word's view mode from Normal to Web Layout.

Changing Your View

This section will show you how to change the Word display; add, split, and switch windows; and set task pane, toolbar, and other display options.

2+ *Show each document in a separate window*
Select Tools → Options, click the View tab, and check the Windows in Taskbar box to show each open document in a different window (this is called the single document interface and it is the default in Word 2002 and 2003).

0+ *Manage multiple windows using the single document interface*
When multiple documents are open, a separate button appears for each on the Windows taskbar. To switch to a particular document, click on its taskbar button. Right-click the button for other window options (Restore, Move, Size, Minimize, Maximize, and Close).

Jump from document to document

Select Window → *document name* to switch to that document.

Press Ctrl-F6 to go to the next open document. Press Ctrl-Shift-F6 to go to the previous open document.

TIP

Windows XP can group multiple open documents under a single Windows taskbar button. To disable this option, select Start → Settings → Control Panel, double-click the Taskbar and Start Menu icon, and uncheck the Group similar taskbar buttons box.

Create an additional window of an open document

Select Window → New Window. Word adds a :1 to the document name in the original window and a :2 to the document name in the new window. You can scroll to different places in each window, view each window in a different view or zoom level, and drag items between the windows. You can make changes to the document in either window.

Split an existing window for two views of a single document

Select Window → Split. The pointer turns into a horizontal gray bar. Pick a spot and click to split the document into two panes, each with its own scroll bars. You can also click and drag the split box just above the single arrow in the vertical scroll bar. To remove a split, select Window → Remove Split.

02+ *Keep the task pane from popping up every time you start Word*

Select Tools → Options, click the View tab, and check the Startup Task Pane box.

Switch between the five basic document views

Select a view from the View menu or click a view button to the left of the horizontal scroll bar. For a description of the views available in different versions of Word, see Part 1.

Set options for using the different views

Tools → Options → View.

In Word 2000-2003, options in the Print and Web Layout section include:

Drawings turns on or off the display of objects created with Word's drawing tools.

Object Anchors indicates the paragraphs to which objects are anchored.

Text Boundaries displays dotted lines on the screen around page margins.

White space between pages (Word 2002 and 2003 only) displays the space between the top of the text and the top edge of the page.

Background colors and images (Word 2003 only) displays colors and images used as a background. These are always visible in Web Layout view; this option also makes them visible (or not) in Print Layout.

Vertical Ruler turns on or off the vertical ruler display.

In Word 2000–2003, the following options are grouped in the Outline and Normal section. In Word 97, they are in different places on the View tab:

Wrap to window wraps text from one line to the next based on the size of the document window rather than on the location of the margins.

Draft font substitutes a single font for all different fonts in a document, speeding up the display of long documents with multiple fonts.

Style area width shows style names to the left of the page margin.

02+ *Open a task pane manually*

Select View → Task Pane. In Word 2003, you can also press Ctrl-F1.

Add or remove a toolbar

Select View → Toolbars and select a toolbar from the list. Or right-click anywhere in the toolbar area and select a toolbar from the pop-up list. To remove a toolbar, simply select it again.

For a list of all available toolbars in Word, select Tools → Customize and click the Toolbars tab.

Hide or show the rulers
    View → Ruler.

Use a heading-based document map to navigate a document

 Select View → Document Map to open a map of headings to the left of the document. Click any heading to jump to that location in the document window.

Get a full-screen view of your documents
    Select View → Full Screen to hide all menus, toolbars, and scroll bars, as well as the status bar. Click the Close Full Screen button on the pop-up command bar or press Esc to exit full-screen mode.

00+ *Preview what a document will look like when published as a web page*
    Select File → Web Page Preview to open your default web browser and display the current document.

Zoom to different levels on a document
    Enter a number in the Zoom box on the Standard toolbar or select a zoom level from the drop-down menu.

    Select View → Zoom to open a dialog box with the same functionality.

Display a document faster by not showing pictures
    Select Tools → Options, click the View tab, and check the Picture placeholders box. In the document, Word displays empty frames instead of pictures. This is only for display purposes. The full pictures are still printed.

02+ *Turn off the smart tags that appear beneath text*
    Select Tools → Options, click the View tab, and check the Smart tags box. Smart tags are pieces of data that

---

Word recognizes as a certain type of data. For example, if you type a person's name and that name also appears as a contact in Microsoft Outlook, Word places a Smart Tag on the name. Clicking the tag provides a limited set of commands for working with the data (such as opening the contact or scheduling a meeting).

Controlling the Flow of a Document

This section will show you how to insert and format breaks, columns, and headers and footers.

Working with Breaks

Show breaks in the document window

In Normal view, page and section breaks show at all times as dashed lines. In Print Layout view (Page Layout view in Word 97), page breaks appear as splits in the pages and no break codes appear. To see actual breaks in Print Layout view, click the Show/Hide button (the paragraph mark) on the Standard toolbar or select Tools → Options, click the View tab, and check the All box.

Insert a manual page break

Select Insert → Break and choose Page Break or press Ctrl-Enter.

Prevent automatic page breaks within paragraphs

Select the paragraph and choose Format → Paragraph, click the Line and Page Breaks tab, and check the Keep lines together box.

Prevent an automatic page break between a paragraph and the following paragraph

Select the first paragraph and choose Format → Paragraph, click the Line and Page Breaks tab, and check the Keep with next box.

Force a page break directly before a paragraph
Select the paragraph and choose Format → Paragraph, click the Line and Page Breaks tab, and check the Page break before box.

Prevent Word from printing the first or last line of a paragraph on a page by itself
Select the paragraph and choose Format → Paragraph, click the Line and Page Breaks tab, and check the Widow/Orphan control box.

00+ *End a line of text and force it to continue beneath an object*
Select Insert → Break and choose Text wrapping break.

Create a new section without starting a new page
Select Insert → Break and choose Continuous.

Insert a break and start the new section on the next page
Select Insert → Break and choose Next page.

Insert a break and start the new section on the next odd- or even-numbered page
Select Insert → Break and choose Even page or Odd page.

Columns

Create or remove columns
Select View → Print Layout (Page Layout in Word 97). Select the text you want to format as a column (or that you want to remove column formatting from), click the Columns button on the Standard toolbar, and select the number of columns you want. Select one column to remove existing columns.

Add a vertical line between columns
Place the insertion point in the section where you want vertical lines between columns. Select Format → Columns and check the Line between box.

Change the width of a column

Place the insertion point in the section where you want to change the width of a column. Drag the column markers on the horizontal ruler to move columns (see Figure 11).

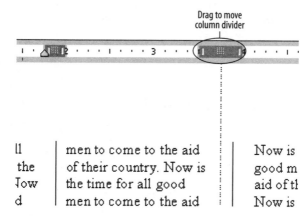

Figure 11. Drag a column handle to size columns

Create a heading that spans multiple columns

Type the heading text at the beginning of the leftmost column and press Enter. Select the heading text, click the Columns button, and make it one column. For a better heading effect, create a border around the new heading paragraph. (See the "Formatting" section in this part.)

Insert a column break to force a new column

Place the insertion point where you want to start the new column. Select Insert → Break, and choose Column break.

Show column boundaries

Select Tools → Options, click the View tab, and check the Text boundaries box. You must be in Print or Web Layout view to see the column boundaries.

Headers and Footers

Edit a header or footer

Select View → Header and Footer. This places you in the header box for the current page (where you can type or insert text and graphics) and opens the Header and Footer toolbar (see Figure 12).

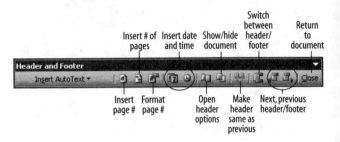

Figure 12. Controlling headers and footers

Insert a chapter number and title into a header or footer

First, you must divide the document into sections—each section represents a chapter. At the beginning of each section, create a heading (using one of the default heading styles) with the chapter number and title. When finished, follow these steps for each chapter:

1. Select View → Header and Footer.

2. Make sure each section is made the same as the previous section (Use the Make header same as previous button).

3. Place the insertion point where you want the chapter number and title to go in the header.

4. Select Insert → Reference → Cross-reference (Insert → Cross- reference in Word 97 and 2000).

5. Select Heading from the Reference type drop-down menu.

6. Select the heading that contains the chapter information from the list in the For which heading box.

7. Select the Heading number from the Insert reference to drop-down list and click the Insert button to insert the chapter number.

8. Select the Heading text from the Insert reference to drop-down list and click the Insert button to insert the chapter title.

Make the first page header or footer different from other pages
Select File → Page Setup, click the Layout tab, and check the Different first page box. Next, go to the first page and create a different header or footer.

Make headers or footers different for odd and even pages
Select File → Page Setup, click the Layout tab, and check the Different odd and even box. Next, create the header for an even page, then an odd page.

Make different headers or footers for each section of a document
Place the insertion point in the section you want to change. Select View → Header and Footer. Click the Same as Previous button on the Header and Footer toolbar to break the connection to the previous section. Edit the header or footer.

Make a header or footer the same as the ones in the previous section
Place the insertion point in the section you want to change. Select View → Header and Footer. Click the Same as Previous button on the Header and Footer toolbar to delete the current header and establish a connection to the previous section.

Adjust the position of a header or footer
To change the distance of a header or footer from the edge of the page, select File → Page Setup, click the Layout tab, and adjust the Header and Footer values. As with all page layout options, you can choose whether

you want to apply the changes to the whole document or from the current point forward (in other words to the current and subsequent sections).

To change the distance of a header or footer from the text on the page, select View → Header and Footer, move to the header or footer you want to adjust, and then use the margin boundaries on the vertical ruler to adjust the size of the header or footer.

Inserting Fields and Reference Items

This section shows you how to insert fields, pictures, diagrams, and other objects, as well as reference items such as a table of contents and an index.

Working with Fields

Insert a field

In Word 2000-2003, select Insert → Field, choose a category and field name from the list, select additional properties, and click the OK button. In Word 2002 and 2003, click the Field Codes button to enter field codes directly.

In Word 97, select Insert → Field and choose a category and field name. Fill in the field codes directly or click Options to set additional properties.

NOTE

The Word help files contain a complete reference of fields and field codes. You can browse their contents using the Help window. In Word 97–2002, you can also right-click any field in the Field dialog box and choose What's This? to jump straight to that field's help file description. Word 2003 no longer includes the What's This? tool.

Edit a field

Right-click the field and choose Edit Field.

NOTE

To edit a field in Word 97 and 2000, you have to toggle the display of the field code (right-click the field and choose Toggle Field Codes) and edit the code manually. It is usually easier to delete the code and insert a new one.

Show the field code instead of the field results

To switch between the results and code for a single field, select the field and press Shift-F9.

To switch between the results and codes for all fields in a document, press Alt-F9.

Shade fields to make them stand out

Select Tools → Options, click the View → tab, and choose Never, Always, or When selected from the Field shading drop-down list.

Lock or unlock a field

Select the field and press Ctrl-Shift-F11. Locking a field prevents its results from being updated.

Update a field

Select the field and press F9 or right-click the field and choose Update Field.

Update all fields in a document

Choose Edit → Select All (or press Ctrl-A), and then press F9.

Have Word automatically update all fields before printing

Select Tools → Options, click the Print tab, and check the Update fields box.

Change a field result to normal text

Select the field and press Ctrl-Shift-F9. This removes the field code, but leaves the result in the document as non-field text.

Footnotes and Endnotes

Insert a footnote or endnote

In Word 2002 and 2003, select Insert → Reference → Footnote, choose Footnote or Endnote and click the Insert button. In Word 97 and 2000, select Insert → Footnote, choose Footnote or Endnote, and click the OK button.

To insert subsequent notes, press Ctrl-Alt-F for footnotes or Ctrl-Alt-D for endnotes.

Change how footnotes or endnotes are numbered

In Word 2002 and 2003, select Insert → Reference → Footnote and choose a new number format from the drop-down list. Next, choose whether to apply the changes to this section or the whole document, and click the Apply button.

In Word 97 and 2000, select Insert → Footnote and click the Options button. Choose a new number format from the drop-down list. Next, choose how to apply numbering. Continuous applies numbering to the whole document—across section and page breaks. You can also have numbering restart at each section or on each page. When you're done, click the OK button.

Change the placement of footnotes or endnotes

In Word 2002 and 2003, select Insert → Reference → Footnote and choose a location from the drop-down list. Next, choose whether to apply the changes to this section or the whole document, and click the Apply button.

In Word 97 and 2000, select Insert → Footnote, click the Options button, choose a location from the drop-down list, and click the OK button.

Quickly view the text of a footnote or endnote

Hold the pointer over the reference mark for a moment to display a pop-up note of text.

Add a footnote or endnote separator

Select View → Normal and then select View → Footnotes (if you have both footnotes and endnotes, Word will ask you which you want to view). In the note area at the bottom of the screen, select Footnote (or Endnote) Separator from the drop-down list.

Add a footnote or endnote continuation notice
Select View → Normal and then select View → Footnotes (if you have both footnotes and endnotes, Word will ask you which you want to view). In the note area at the bottom of the screen, select Footnote (or Endnote) Continuation Notice from the drop-down list and enter the text that should appear when a footnote or endnote continues onto another page.

Delete a footnote or endnote
Select the reference mark, and then press Backspace or Delete. Word renumbers the remaining notes.

Move a footnote or endnote
Select the reference mark and use any method to move or copy the note to its new location. Word renumbers the notes if necessary.

Convert a footnote to an endnote or vice versa
In Print Layout view, right-click the footnote or endnote at the bottom of the page and choose Convert to Endnote (or Footnote). In Normal view, select View → Footnotes, right-click the footnote or endnote and choose Convert to Endnote (or Footnote).

Convert all footnotes to endnotes or vice versa
Select Insert → Reference → Footnote and click the Convert button. In Word 97 and 2000, select Insert → Footnote, click the Options button, and then click the Convert button.

Use the same footnote or endnote more than once
Select Insert → Reference → Cross-reference (Insert → Cross-reference in Word 97 and 2000). In the Reference type box, choose Footnote (or Endnote) from the drop-down list. In the For which footnote (or endnote) box, choose the note you want to refer to. In the Insert reference

to box, choose Footnote (or Endnote) number from the
drop-down list. Finally, click the Insert button.

Cross-References, Captions, and Bookmarks

Create a cross-reference to another item in a document
Select Insert → Reference → Cross-reference (Insert →
Cross-reference in Word 97 and 2000). Choose the type
of item you want to refer to—Footnote, Heading, Figure, etc.—from the Reference type drop-down list. In the
Insert reference to box, choose the information you want
inserted in the document from the drop-down list—for
example, the Footnote number. Finally, pick the exact
reference target from the list at the bottom of the dialog
box and click the Insert button.

Change the target of a cross-reference
Click the cross-reference field and select Insert → Refer-
ence → Cross-reference (Insert → Cross-reference in
Word 97 and 2000). Choose a new reference target from
the list at the bottom of the dialog box and click the
Insert button.

Update cross-references in a document
If the cross-reference refers to a specific location in the
document (e.g., "see page 45") and the page number
changes, right-click the cross-reference field and select
Update Field. Or click the cross-reference field and press
F9.

To update all cross-references in a document, choose
Edit → Select All or press Ctrl-A and then press F9.

Add a caption to a table, figure, or other object
Select the item and choose Insert → Reference → Caption (Insert → Caption in Word 97 and 2000) or right-
click the item and choose Caption from the shortcut
menu. Enter your text in the Caption box, and choose a
label (Figure, Table, Equation, etc) from the drop-down

list. Finally, choose whether to position the text above or below the selected item, and click the OK button.

Have Word automatically add captions when you insert objects

Select Insert → Reference → Caption (Insert → Caption in Word 97 and 2000) and click the AutoCaption button. Check the box next to the items that should automatically get captions, choose a label and position for each item, and click the OK button.

Change a caption label

Delete the existing caption (by selecting it and pressing Delete or Backspace) and insert a new caption (see the first task in this section).

Change all similar caption labels

Select one of the captions you want to change and choose Insert → Reference → Caption (Insert → Caption in Word 97 and 2000). Choose a new label from the Label drop-down list and click the OK button.

Change the numbering of captions

Select a caption, then choose Insert → Reference → Caption (Insert → Caption in Word 97 and 2000) and click the Numbering button. Choose a new number format from the Format drop-down list and click the OK button.

Include a chapter number in a caption

First, you must create a section for each chapter and format the chapter title using one of Word's built-in heading styles. Then select Insert → Reference → Caption (Insert → Caption in Word 97 and 2000), click the Numbering button, and check the Include chapter number box.

Create a table of figures using captions in the document

Select Insert → Reference → Index and Tables (Insert → Index and Tables in Word 97 and 2000) and click the Table of Figures tab.

Add a bookmark
> Place the insertion point or make a selection and then select Insert → Bookmark. Bookmarks are used to mark locations for future reference.

Delete a bookmark
> Select Insert → Bookmark; choose a bookmark and click the Delete button.

Go to a bookmark
> Select Insert → Bookmark; choose a bookmark and click the Go To button.
>
> Select Edit → Go To or press Ctrl-G and choose Bookmarks from the Go to what list. Next, select a specific bookmark from the Enter bookmark name drop-down list and click the Go To button.

`00+` *Show or hide bookmarks in a document*
> Select Tools → Options, click the View tab, and check the Bookmarks box. Bookmarks are shown with light gray brackets around them.

Tables and Indexes

Create a table of contents
> Place the insertion point where you want to insert the table of contents and select Insert → Reference → Index and Tables (Insert → Index and Tables in Word 97 and 2000), click the Table of Contents tab, and click the OK button. Word inserts the table of contents as a single field based on the headings in your document.

Make a table of contents use some heading levels, but not others
> In Word 2002 and 2003, select Insert → Reference → Index and Tables, click the Table of Contents tab, and click the Options button. Next, check the Styles box and uncheck the Outline levels box. Enter the table of contents level for each heading level you want to use and leave the others empty. For example, to skip headings formatted with the Heading 1 style, leave the box blank

and enter a "1" in the box for the Heading 2 style, "2" in the box for the Heading 3 style, and so on.

In Word 97 and 2000, select Insert → Index and Tables, click the Table of Contents tab, and click the Options button. Check the Styles box and enter the table of contents levels as outlined above.

Update a table of contents
Select the table and press F9.

To update a table of contents automatically before printing, select Tools → Options, click the Print tab, and check the Update fields box.

Make the table of contents appear instead of {TOC}
This happens when the field code is displayed instead of the field results. Right-click the field and choose Toggle Field Codes.

Mark a special entry to be included in a table of contents, even if it's not a heading

Select the entry and press Alt-Shift-O. Enter a name in the Entry box and choose the level at which the entry should appear. If your document has more than one table of contents, choose which table you want the entry to appear in from the Table identifier drop-down list.

When you create the table of contents, select Insert → Reference → Indexes and Tables (Insert → Index and Tables in Word 97 and 2000), click the Table of Contents tab, click the Options button, and make sure you check the Table entry fields box (table entry fields are the special entries you marked; if you don't select it, Word only includes headings in the table).

Delete a table of contents
Select the table of contents and press Delete or Backspace.

In Word 2002 and 2003, from Outline View (View →
Outline), you can also click the Go to TOC button on
the Outlining toolbar and then press Delete.

Fix page numbers and missing headings in my table of contents
These problems usually occur when a document has
been changed and the table of contents has not been
updated. Select the table and press F9.

Change the format used in my table of contents
The best way to change a table of contents is to delete it
and build a new one.

You can also change the formatting styles used in a table
of contents. In Word 2002 and 2003, choose Format
→ Styles and Formatting and then click a line in the table
of contents near the number. A TOC style (TOC1,
TOC2, etc.) appears in the Formatting of Selected Text
box. Right-click the style and choose Modify.

In Word 97 and 2000, use Format → Styles → Modify.

Mark a citation for use in a table of authorities
A table of authorities lists the references in a legal document. To create a table of authorities, you must mark
citations in the document and then build the table. To
mark a citation, do the following:

1. Select the first long citation in your document and
   press Alt-Shift-I.

2. In the Selected text box, change the long citation to
   appear the way you want it in the table of authorities.

3. Assign the citation a category (Cases, Statutes, Treaties, etc) from the Category drop-down list.

4. In the Short citation box, enter the short version for
   the citation that is used in the rest of the document.

5. Click the Mark button to mark a single citation or
   the Mark All button to mark all citations that match
   the text in the Short citation box.

Remove a citation from a table of authorities

Click the Show/Hide button on the Standard toolbar to show field codes. To the right of a citation, you'll see a TA field (e.g., { TA \s "*citation*" }). Delete the entire field.

Create a table of authorities using marked citations

Place the insertion point where you want to build the table. Select Insert → Reference → Index and Tables (Insert → Index and Tables in Word 97 and 2000) and click the Table of Authorities tab.

Update a table of authorities

Select the table and press F9.

To update the table automatically before printing, select Tools → Options, click the Print tab, and check the Update fields box.

Create or modify categories of citations

Press Alt-Shift-I, click the Category button, and choose a category (Cases, Statutes, Treaties, etc) from the Category drop-down list. Enter a name in the Replace with box and click the OK button.

Create an index

Place the insertion point where the index will go and select Insert → Reference → Index and Tables (Insert → Index and Tables in Word 97 and 2000) and click the Index tab. Select configuration options and click the OK button.

Mark a selection to be included in an index

Select a word or phrase and press Alt-Shift-X. In the Main entry box, type the entry as it should appear in the index. Enter text in the Subentry box to mark the selection as a subentry in the index. Choose whether the page number for the entry should be boldfaced or italicized and click the Mark button. Click the Mark All button to mark all instances of the word the same way.

To create an index entry without using pre-selected text, just place the insertion point and press Alt-Shift-X.

Mark long entries (more than one page) to be included in an index

Select the text and choose Insert → Bookmark. Then press Alt-Shift-X, and select the Page range option. Choose the bookmark you just created from the drop-down list and click the Mark button.

Create an index entry that refers to another entry

Press Alt-Shift-X and select the Cross-reference option. Enter the text for the cross-reference (e.g., "See Bicycle") and click the Mark button.

Change how a marked entry will appear in the index

Index entries are marked by placing a field to the right of the marked phrase (e.g., { XE "Bicycle:Repair" }). If you don't see the fields, click the Show/Hide button on the Standard toolbar. Select the text inside the quotes and replace or format it to change the index entry.

Delete an index entry

Select the entire index field to the right of the marked phrase and delete it. If you don't see the field, click the Show/Hide button on the Standard toolbar.

Modify the styles used for entries in an index

Select Insert → Reference → Index and Tables (Insert → Index and Tables in Word 97 and 2000), click the Index tab, and click the Modify button.

Have Word automatically mark index entries using a concordance file

A *concordance file* is a separate document used to create an automatic index (an example would be a list of words for use in indexes for all documents of a particular type or created in a particular department). The document contains a table with two columns. The first column lists the word or phrases you want Word to search for in your document. The second column lists the entries you want

Word to enter in the index when it finds the phrase. Create a new file, create the table, and then save the file.

In the document you want to index, select Insert → Reference → Index and Tables (Insert → Index and Tables in Word 97 and 2000), click the Index tab, and click the AutoMark button. Select the concordance file and click the Open button. Word searches the document for any matching phrases and marks the first occurrence as an index entry.

Working with Hyperlinks

Create a hyperlink

Select the text or object, or just place the insertion point, and select Insert → Hyperlink (or press Ctrl-K). In the Link to list on the lefthand side, choose a target (Existing File or Web Page, Place in This Document, Create New Document, or Email Address). Configure the hyperlink and click the OK button.

Remove a hyperlink, but keep the text

In Word 2002 and 2003, right-click the hyperlink and select Remove Hyperlink.

In Word 2000, right-click the hyperlink and select Hyperlink → Remove Hyperlink.

In Word 97, right-click the hyperlink and select Hyperlink → Edit Hyperlink and click the Remove Link button.

Change a hyperlink

Right-click the hyperlink and choose Edit Hyperlink (or Hyperlink → Edit Hyperlink in Word 97). Modify the hyperlink (or type in a new one) and click the OK button.

Follow a hyperlink found in a document

In Word 2002 and 2003, hold down the Ctrl key and click the link.

In Word 97 and 2000, click the link.

Change how hyperlinks are followed
> Select Tools → Options, click the Edit tab, and uncheck the Use Ctrl+Click to follow hyperlink box. Now you can follow a hyperlink just by clicking it.

Set a hyperlink base that all hyperlinks in a document will use
> Select File → Properties, click on the Summary tab, and type a base in the Hyperlink base box. A hyperlink base is a base path or URL used for all hyperlinks in a document. The hyperlink base lets you create relative links in the document that specify the path and name of the linked file, but only within the hyperlink base. If the main location (or domain name) change later, it is easier to move the structure intact and change only the hyperlink base instead of changing the individual hyperlinks throughout the documents on the site.

Inserting Objects

The following tasks show you how to insert objects into your document, including pictures, drawings, charts, and information from other types of documents.

Clip Art, Drawings, and Pictures

Insert a piece of clip art
> Select Insert → Picture → ClipArt.
>
> In Word 2003, the Clip Art task pane opens. Enter a part of the filename in the Search for box and click the Go button. Use the Search in and Results should be drop-down menus to specify where to search and the types of files to search for. Word displays thumbnails of the results. If you see one you like, double-click it to insert it in your document or click the down arrow that appears when you hover your pointer over the thumbnail to reveal additional options.

In Word 2002, the Insert Clip Art task pane opens. Enter a part of the filename in the Search text box and click the Search button. The Other Search Options section lets you specify where to search and the types of files to search for. By default, the search returns clip art, pictures, video, and sound files. Insert clip art the same way as in Word 2003.

In Word 97 and 2000, the Insert Clip Art dialog box opens with tools for finding and inserting clip art. Browse through the categories of clip art and when you find one, click the thumbnail to reveal a pop-up menu with options for inserting and manipulating the art.

Use the Clip Organizer to browse clip art and other media
In Word 2002 and 2003, select Insert → Picture → ClipArt and click the Clip Organizer link. In Word 97 and 2000, select Insert → Picture → Clip Art. Select a folder from the collection list to see thumbnail previews in the right pane.

Add a clip to the Clip Organizer
In Word 2002 and 2003, select Insert → Picture → ClipArt and click the Organize clips link (Clip Organizer link in Word 2002). In the Clip Organizer window, select File → Add Clips to Organizer → On my own. Find the clip and click the Add button or the Add to button to specify where the clip should be catalogued.

In Word 97 and 2000, select Insert → Picture → Clip Art and click the Import Clips button. Select the clips you want to add and click the Import button.

View the properties and a preview of a clip before you insert it
In Word 2002 and 2003, click the down arrow on the clip's thumbnail and choose Preview/Properties.

In Word 97 and 2000, right-click a clip's thumbnail and choose Clip Properties. In the dialog box, click the Preview button to preview the clip.

00+ *Find more clips online*

Select Insert → Picture → ClipArt and click the Clip art on Office Online link (Clips Online link in Word 2002 and Clips Online button in Word 2000). This opens Microsoft's Design Gallery in your default web browser.

Insert a picture from a file

Select Insert → Picture → From File, locate the file, and click the Insert button. This action embeds the picture, which increases the document's size.

Link a picture to a file

Select Insert → Picture → From File and locate the file. In Word 2000-2003, click the down arrow next to the Insert button, and choose Link to File. In Word 97, check the Link to file box and click the Insert button. The picture is displayed, but not embedded. Changes to the original picture file are reflected in the document.

Retrieve a picture from a scanner or camera

Select Insert → Picture → From Scanner or Camera.

Create an organizational chart

In Word 2002 and 2003, select Insert → Picture → Organization Chart or select Insert → Diagram and choose Organization Chart from the diagram type box. This creates a basic hierarchical organization chart and opens an Organization Chart toolbar (see Figure 13).

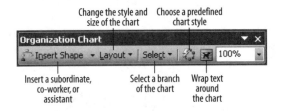

Figure 13. Creating an organization chart

In Word 97 and 2000, select Insert → Object, click the Create New tab, select Organization Chart from the Object type box, and click the OK button.

Create a diagram

Select Insert → Diagram and select a basic diagram (cycle, pyramid, target, and so on). Use the Diagram toolbar to change styles and add shapes.

Create another type of drawing or picture

Select Insert → Picture → New Drawing. Use the Drawing toolbar (see Figure 14) to add components to a blank drawing canvas.

Figure 14. Use the Drawing toolbar to create many different elements

Numbered items in this list correspond to elements in the figure.

1. Holds commands for grouping, ordering, arranging, and moving shapes in the drawing.

2. Provides a pointer for selecting shapes.

3. Inserts various types of predefined shapes (lines, arrows, flowchart symbols). It works the same as the Insert → Picture → AutoShapes command.

4. Line tool

5. Arrow tool

6. Rectangle tool

7. Circle tool

8. Inserts a text box.

9. Inserts WordArt (predefined shapes and shadows applied to your own text). It works the same as the Insert → Picture → WordArt command.

10. Inserts a diagram or organization chart (same as Insert → Diagram or Insert → Picture → Organization chart).

11. Same as the Insert → Picture → ClipArt command.

12. Same as the Insert → Picture → From File command.

13. Changes the fill color for the selected object.

14. Changes the line color for the selected object.

15. Changes text color.

16. Changes line style.

17. Changes dash style.

18. Changes arrow style.

19. Changes shadowing of selected object.

20. Changes 3-D effect of selected object.

02+ *Specify whether Word automatically inserts a drawing canvas around AutoShapes*

Select Tools → Options, click the General tab, and check the Automatically create drawing canvas when inserting AutoShapes box.

Create a chart based on a datasheet of information

Select Insert → Picture → Chart. Word inserts a chart object and opens a separate window with a datasheet. Fill out the data (or change or add headings) to update the chart. If you close the datasheet, you can double-click the chart at any time to reactivate it. You can also select the chart and choose the following commands:

- View → Datasheet to reopen the separate datasheet window

- Insert → Cells to create new cells in the datasheet

- The Format menu lets you change the font, number style, and placement of the chart

- Tools → Options changes very basic datasheet and chart settings
- Chart → Chart Type lets you select the type of chart (bar, pie, line, etc.)
- Chart → Chart Options lets you change titles, axes, gridlines, legends, and data labels

---

TIP

Looking for a better solution? Create a worksheet and chart in Excel and then insert it into Word. This is covered a bit later in this part.

Text Boxes

Create a text box

Text boxes are floating objects that contain text. In Word 2000–2003, select Insert → Text Box or click the Text Box button on the Drawing toolbar. In Word 97, there is no menu command; you must draw the text box by dragging.

Create a text box around existing text

Select the text and choose Insert → Text Box.

Link a text box to another text box to continue a story

Select the first text box, click the Create Text Box Link button on the Text Box toolbar, and then click another empty text box. Text that does not fit into the first text box is automatically continued in the next linked text box. You can link any number of text boxes in this manner. Use the Next and Previous Text Box buttons on the Text Box toolbar to move between linked text boxes.

Break the link between two text boxes

Select a text box and click the Break Forward Link button on the Text Box toolbar to break any links from the current text box.

Convert a text box to a frame

Select the text box and choose Format → Text Box, click the Text Box tab, and click the Convert to Frame button. This converts the text box from a floating object on the drawing layer to a framed object in the text layer (see "How a Document Works" in Part 1).

Change the direction of text in a text box

Select the text box and click the Change Text Direction button on the Text Box toolbar.

Move a text box

Click the Select Objects button on the Drawing toolbar to make the selection pointer active. Position the pointer on the outer edge of the text box so that the pointer becomes a four-way arrow. Click and drag the text box into position.

Or, select the text box by clicking its outer edge (not the items within the text box). Use the arrow keys to make large movements. Hold down the Ctrl key while using the arrow keys to slightly nudge the text box.

Manipulating Objects

Change the size of an object

Click the Select Objects button on the Drawing toolbar to make the selection pointer active. Select the object and use the drag handles at the corners and sides of the object.

To specify an exact size, select the object and choose Format → *objectname* and click the Size tab.

Change the wrapping style of an object
> Select the object and choose Format → *objectname*, and click the Layout tab (in Word 97, choose Format → *objectname* → Wrapping).

Change the cropping for a picture object
> Select the object and choose Format → Picture, click the Picture tab, and use the controls in the Crop from section.

Change the color display settings for a picture object
> Select the object and choose Format → Picture, click the Picture tab, and use the controls in the Image control section.

2+ *Change the resolution for a picture object*
> Select the object and choose Format → Picture, click the Picture tab, and click the Compress button.

2+ *Turn on compression for a picture object*
> Select the object and choose Format → Picture, click the Picture tab, click the Compress button, and check the Compress pictures box.

Change the fill and line colors for a drawing object
> Select the object and choose Format → Picture and click the Colors and Lines tab.

0+ *Add alternative web text for an object*
> Select the object and choose Format → Object and click the Web tab. Enter your text in the Alternative text box and click the OK button.

Embedding and Linking

Insert a file into a document
> Select Insert → File; choose a file and click the Insert button. The file is embedded in the Word document. This command is best for inserting the contents of another Word file. If you insert a non-Word file, the information

in the file is converted (if a converter is available) into the Word format.

Embed an object from another file

Select Insert → Object, click the Create from File tab, type or browse for the filename, and click the OK button. The entire contents of the file are embedded into the Word document as a single object.

You can also copy an object from another open document and paste the object into an open Word document.

Create a new object

Select Insert → Object, click the Create New tab, choose an object type, and click the OK button. Double-click the object to edit it.

Drag objects or information between programs

Drag the selection (e.g., an Excel graph) into an open Word document to move it. Hold down the Ctrl key while dragging to copy the selection. What happens next depends on the program. If you drag a chart from Excel, Word treats the chart as a picture. If, however, you drag a spreadsheet from Excel, Word treats it as a table.

Edit an embedded object from Word

Double-click the object to edit it using commands from the object's source application. For example, if you double-click an object inserted from an Excel document, you can access Excel's menus for working with the object.

Link an object to another file

When you link an object, it is displayed in the Word document, but not embedded. If the original object (say, an Excel chart) is updated, the updates are reflected in the Word document.

To link an entire file, select Insert → Object, click the Create from File tab, choose the file, check the Link to file box, and click the OK button.

To link to a particular object, open the source file, copy the object, switch to the Word document, select Edit → Paste Special, and choose the Paste link option.

Edit a linked object
Double-click the linked object to open the source file in the application used to create it.

Update a linked object manually
Select Edit → Links, select the links you want to update, and click the Update Now button.

Stop a linked object from updating automatically
Select Edit → Links, select the link, and choose the Manual update option.

Prevent a linked object from being updated
Select Edit → Links, select the link, and check the Locked box.

Break the link for a linked object
Select Edit → Links, select the link, and click the Break Link button.

Reconnect a linked object after breaking it
You must insert the linked object again.

Have Word update linked objects automatically when I print a document
Select Tools → Options, click the Print tab, and check the Update links box.

Working with Tables

This section shows you how to create and edit tables. You will learn how to resize, insert, remove, and format columns and rows.

Create a quick table by choosing the number of rows and columns
Click the Insert Table button on the Standard toolbar and select the number of rows and columns. To create

more rows and columns than shown, hold the mouse button down and drag to select the size of the table.

Draw a table to fit a particular space

Select Table → Draw Table to change the pointer to the table drawing tool. Drag a rectangle to make the outer border of your table. Drag lines inside the border to form cells. This is a quick way to make irregular tables.

Create a table using other options

Select Table → Insert → Table, choose the number of rows and columns, how the contents should fit, and click the OK button.

Create a single row table by typing out a line of columns

Type a plus sign (+) followed by hyphens (-). Type an additional plus sign for each column marker and a final plus sign for the right border of the table. For example, type

"+--------------+---------------+-------------+"

and press Enter to create a table with a single row and three roughly equal columns.

If this doesn't work, select Tools → AutoCorrect Options (Tools → AutoCorrect in Word 97 and 2000), click the AutoFormat As You Type tab, and check the Tables box.

Insert columns or rows into an existing table

In Word 2000–2003, place the insertion point somewhere in the table. Choose Table → Insert and then pick one of the column or row options.

In Word 97, these commands appear right on the Table menu. Place the insertion point somewhere in the table and select Table → Insert Row or Table → Insert Column.

Insert cells into an existing table

    Place the insertion point somewhere in the table and select Table → Insert → Cells. Choose how to shift the existing cells in the table and click the OK button.

Remove columns, rows, or cells from a table

    In Word 2000–2003, place the insertion point in the column, row, or cell you want to remove, select Table → Delete, and choose Columns, Rows, or Cells. You can also select a group of cells and press Backspace or select Edit → Cut.

    In Word 97, select the column, row, or cell to delete and choose the appropriate command from the Table menu.

Delete the text in a group of cells without removing the cells

    Drag to select the cells and press Delete. Do not press Backspace as this will delete the cells themselves.

Select an entire column or row

    Place the insertion point in the column or row and choose Table → Select → Column or Table → Select → Row (Table → Select Column or Table → Select Row in Word 97).

    Move the pointer to the top edge of the column (it turns into a down-pointing arrow) or to the left edge of a row (it turns into an upper-right-pointing arrow) and click to select the column or row.

Select a cell or group of cells

    Place the insertion point in the cell and choose Table → Select → Cell (Table → Select Cell in Word 97).

    Or move the pointer over the left edge of the cell (it turns into an upper-right-pointing arrow) and click to select the cell.

    Drag to select a group of cells.

Select an entire table
> Place the insertion point anywhere in the table and choose Table → Select → Table (Table → Select Table in Word 97).

Merge multiple cells into a single cell
> Select the cells and choose Table → Merge Cells.

Split a cell or cells into multiple cells
> Place the insertion point in the cell (or select a group of cells) and choose Table → Split Cell. Choose the number of rows and columns into which to split the cell.

Split a table
> Place the insertion point in the row that will become the top line of the second table and select Table → Split Table.

Format a table automatically
> In Word 2002 and 2003, select Table → Table AutoFormat, choose a Category, a Table style, check any additional options, and click the Apply button.
>
> In Word 2000 and 97, select Table → Table AutoFormat, choose a Format, check any additional options, and click the OK button.

Make a group of rows or columns a uniform size
> Select a group of cells in the row or column and choose Table → AutoFit → Distribute Rows Evenly or Table → AutoFit → Distribute Columns Evenly (Table → Distribute Rows Evenly or Table → Distribute Columns Evenly in Word 97).

00+ *Make a table expand automatically to fit the contents of the table*
> Select Table → AutoFit → AutoFit to Contents.

00+ *Make a table contract to fit the window whenever the window changes*
> Select Table → AutoFit → AutoFit to Window.

Make the headings of the table repeat on the first line if the table crosses a page break

Select Table → Heading Rows Repeat (Table → Headings in Word 97).

00+ *Convert a table to text*

Select Table → Convert → Table to Text, choose how you want to separate the text (Paragraph marks, Commas, Tabs, Other), and click the OK button.

Convert text to a table

Select the text you want to convert and then choose Table → Convert → Text to Table (Table → Text to Table in Word 97), enter the number of columns and rows, choose an AutoFit behavior option, and specify where each new cell begins (Paragraph, Comma, Tab, Other), and click the OK button.

Sort a table

Select Table → Sort; you can sort by up to three columns in a nested sort.

Change the orientation of text in a cell

Right-click the cell and choose Text Direction. You can also select a cell and click the Change Text Direction button on the Tables and Borders toolbar.

Create a formula that uses values in other cells

Place the insertion point in a cell and select Table → Formula. Type in a formula or select one from the Paste function drop-down list, choose a number format, and click the OK button.

Hide the gridlines in a table

Select Table → Hide Gridlines.

00+ *Specify an exact size and alignment for a table*

Select Table → Table Properties and click the Table tab or right-click the table, choose Table Properties and click the Table tab. Enter a size, choose an alignment, and click the OK button.

00+ *Make text wrap around a table*

    Select Table → Table Properties, click the Table tab, and choose the Around option in the Text wrapping section of the dialog box.

Specify an exact size and alignment for a cell

    In Word 2000-2003, select Table → Table Properties and click the Cell tab. Enter a size, choose an alignment, and click the OK button.

    In Word 97, select Table → Cell Height and Width. Enter a size, choose an alignment, and click the OK button.

00+ *Change the margins for a specific table cell*

    Select Table → Table Properties, click the Cell tab; click the Options button; uncheck the Same as the whole table box; enter values for the top, bottom, left, and right margins; and click the OK button.

00+ *Change the default margins for all table cells*

    Select Table → Table Properties; click the Table tab; click the Options button; enter values for the top, bottom, left, and right margins; and click the OK button.

00+ *Change the space between table cells*

    Select Table → Table Properties, click the Table tab, click the Options button, check the Allow spacing between cells box, enter a value, and click the OK button.

Specify an exact size for each column in a table

    Place the insertion point in a column. In Word 2000-2003, select Table → Table Properties, click the Column tab, check the Preferred width box, enter a value, and click the OK button. Use the Previous and Next Column buttons to set each column while the dialog box is still open.

    In Word 97, select Table → Cell Height and Width and click the Column tab. Enter an exact size and click the OK button. Use the Previous and Next Column buttons to set each column while the dialog box is still open.

Specify an exact size for each row in a table

Place the insertion point in a row. In Word 2002 and 2003, select Table → Table Properties, click the Row tab, check the Specify height box, enter a value, and click the OK button. Use the Previous and Next Row buttons to set each row while the dialog box is still open.

In Word 97, select Table → Cell Height and Width and click the Row tab. Enter an exact size and click the OK button. Use the Previous and Next Row buttons to set each row while the dialog box is still open.

Prevent a row from breaking across a page

Select Table → Table Properties (Table → Cell Height and Width in Word 97), click the Row tab, and uncheck the Allow row to break across pages box.

Spelling and Other Tools

This section shows you how to use Word's spelling, grammar, and research tools. You also learn how to hyphenate documents, print envelopes and labels, and work with XML.

Spelling and Grammar

Review misspelled words in the document window

By default, squiggly red lines appear under suspect words in the document window. Right-click the word to see spelling suggestions. Double-click the Spelling and Grammar Status icon (looks like a book) on the Status bar to jump to the next misspelled word and view a shortcut menu with spelling suggestions.

> **Turn off the red and green lines under words**
>
> Select Tools → Options (or right-click the Spelling and Grammar Status icon on the Status bar and choose Options) and click the Spelling & Grammar tab. Check the Hide spelling errors in this document box and the Hide grammatical errors in this document box.

Turn off background spelling and grammar check

Select Tools → Options, click the Spelling & Grammar tab, and uncheck the Check spelling as you type box and the Check grammar as you type box.

Perform a full spelling and grammar check

Select Tools → Spelling and Grammar or press F7 to open the Spelling and Grammar dialog box (see Figure 15), which shows errors in context along with suggested corrections.

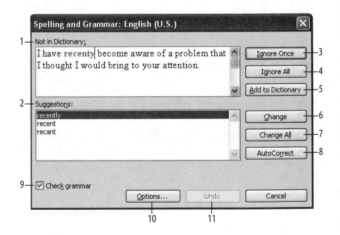

Figure 15. Check spelling and grammar for an entire document at once

Numbered items in this list correspond to elements in the figure.

1. *Not in Dictionary*. The name of this window changes based on the error found. "Not in Dictionary" is displayed for spelling errors. For grammatical errors, Word displays the type of error found, such as "Passive voice" or "Repeated space." Spelling errors are indicated in red text, grammatical errors in green. Use the buttons on the right to act on the error. To apply custom corrections, type a change directly in this window and click the Change button.

2. *Suggestions*. This holds suggested corrections for the error. Select a suggestion and click the Change or Change All button (see #6 and 7).

3. *Ignore*. Click this button to ignore the current instance of the error. The next time you check the document, Word displays the error again.

4. *Ignore All (Ignore Rule)*. With spelling errors, clicking the Ignore All button causes Word to ignore *all* instances of the error in the document. The next time you check the document, however, Word displays the errors again.

   The button changes to Ignore Rule when a grammatical error is encountered. Click it and Word will ignore the grammatical rule throughout the document and in all *future* checks of the document, as well. Select Tools → Options, click the Spelling & Grammar tab, and click the Recheck Document button to reset the rules for a document.

5. *Add to Dictionary (Next Sentence)*. If the word is not misspelled, but simply not recognized by Word's dictionary, add it to the dictionary by clicking the Add

to Dictionary button. Additions to the dictionary are stored in a file called *custom.dic* by default.

For grammatical errors, the button changes to Next Sentence, which skips the current error and resumes checking with the next sentence. Click this button or the Change button to enter a custom correction in the error window.

6. *Change*. Select a correction in the Suggestions window or enter a custom correction in the error window and then click the Change button.

7. *Change All*. Available only with spelling errors, this button changes all instances of the error in the document to the selected suggestion.

8. *AutoCorrect*. This button adds the misspelled word and the selected correction to the AutoCorrect list. If Word encounters the same error in a document, it corrects the error as soon as it's typed.

9. *Check Grammar*. Check this box if you want Word to check for grammatical errors.

10. *Options*. Click this button to view the Spelling & Grammar tab.

11. *Undo*. Click this button to reverse the last correction made.

Check only spelling errors

Select Tools → Spelling and Grammar and uncheck the Check grammar box.

Create a custom dictionary

Select Tools → Options, click the Spelling & Grammar tab, click the Custom Dictionaries button (Dictionaries button in Word 97 and 2000), and then click the New button. Name the dictionary file and click the OK button. Word creates a text file with a *.dic* extension. You can then open that file in Word and enter dictionary entries manually or add them automatically while spell-checking documents.

Add an existing custom dictionary
Select Tools → Options, click the Spelling & Grammar tab, click the Custom Dictionaries button (Dictionaries button in Word 97 and 2000), and then click the Add button. In the dialog box, browse to a dictionary file and click the OK button to add it to the list of custom dictionaries available in Word.

Remove a custom dictionary
Select Tools → Options, click the Spelling & Grammar tab, click the Custom Dictionaries button (Dictionaries button in Word 97 and 2000), select a custom dictionary, and click the Remove button.

Change what the grammar checker looks for
Select Tools → Options, click the Spelling & Grammar tab, and click the Settings button. Choose a writing style (Casual, Standard, Formal, Technical, or Other), select your options, and click the OK button.

Recheck a document where you have previously ignored words
Select Tools → Options, click the Spelling & Grammar tab, and click the Recheck Document button.

Spell-check numbers, Internet addresses, and words in upper case
Select Tools → Options, click the Spelling & Grammar tab, and use the options in the Spelling section of the dialog box.

Show the readability statistics for a document
Select Tools → Options, click the Spelling & Grammar tab, and check the Show readability statistics box. Next, select Tools → Spelling and Grammar and do a full spell-check of the document. The statistics are displayed at the end of the spell-check. This option is unavailable if grammar checking is turned off. A sample Readability Statistics dialog box for Part 1 of this book is shown in Figure 16.

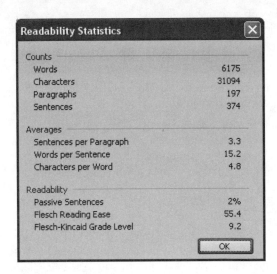

Figure 16. Readability statistics show interesting grammatical information

Research Services

03+ *Research a word or phrase*

Select Tools → Research, type a word in the Search for box, and press Enter to search all available research services (dictionary, thesaurus, translation, and any others you installed).

Select a word or phrase in a document and then select Tools → Research (or Alt-Left Click a selection or word).

03+ *Look up a word in the dictionary*

Select Tools → Research, type a word in the Search for box (or use a word you already selected), select a dictionary from the drop-down list, and press Enter.

Look up alternative words in the thesaurus

In Word 2002 and 2003, select Tools → Language → Thesaurus (or press Shift-F7). If a word was selected, synonyms are listed. If no word was selected, type a word in the Search for box and press Enter. Click the down arrow next to the desired synonym and choose Insert.

In Word 97 and 2000, select a word and choose Tools → Language → Thesaurus (or press Shift-F7). Select a synonym and click the Replace button. You can also type a word in the Replace with Synonym box and click the Look Up button.

3+ *Add or change research services*

Select Tools → Research and click the Research options link. Select from the available services or click the Add Services button to enter the URL for a service provider.

XML

2+ *Save a document as XML*

Select File → Save As and choose XML Document from the Save as type drop-down menu.

NOTE

XML is a document format where elements of the document are represented by customized tags. XML allows a standardization of document definition, transmission, validation, and interpretation across platforms. All versions of Microsoft Office 2003 (and the standalone version of Word 2003) let you save a document in XML format. Advanced XML features (those described in the rest of this section) are available only in Microsoft Office 2003 Professional Edition and are intended mainly for document format designers and developers.

? *Add or remove XML schemas for a document*

Select Tools → Templates and Add-Ins and click the XML Schema tab. Click Add schema to locate and attach an XML schema document to the current Word document. Use the checkboxes next to the schemas listed to select whether each schema is currently applied.

03+ *Show XML tags in a document*

Select View → Task Pane, click the down-pointing arrow at the top of the pane, and choose XML Structure. Check the Show XML tags in the document box. You can also press Ctrl-Shift-X to toggle this option on or off.

03+ *Print XML tags along with a document*

Select Tools → Options, click the Print, tab, and check the XML tags box.

03+ *Apply an XML tag*

Select the content you want to tag. Select View → Task Pane, click the down-pointing arrow at the top of the pane, and choose XML Structure. Select an element from the Choose an element to apply to your current selection box. Some elements also let you specify specific attributes.

03+ *Remove an XML tag*

Press Ctrl-Shift-X until you can see XML tags in the document. In the document window, right-click a Start of *Tag Name* or End of *Tag Name* element and choose Remove *Tag Name* tag.

03+ *Set advanced XML options*

Select Tools → Templates and Add-Ins, click the XML Schema tab, and click the XML Options button.

03+ *Have Word validate XML against attached schemas*

Select Tools → Templates and Add-Ins, click the XML Schema tab, and check the Validate document against attached schemas box.

03+ *Attach XML expansion packs to a document*

Select Tools → Templates and Add-Ins and click the XML Expansion Packs tab. Select an expansion pack and click the Add button.

Other Tools

Translate a document or selection
Select Tools → Language → Translate. Enter text, use the current selection, or select the entire document. Choose the languages you want to translate and click the Go button.

Calculate the word and character count for a document
Select Tools → Word Count to view statistics for the entire document. You can also calculate the word and character count for a specific selection.

See the word count on a toolbar

Select View → Toolbars → Word Count and click the Recount button to display a current word count for the document or selection.

Automatically create a summary of a document
Select Tools → AutoSummarize, choose a type of summary, the length of the summary, and click the OK button.

Hyphenation

Turn on automatic hyphenation
Select Tools → Language → Hyphenation and check the Automatically hyphenate document box.

Control options for automatic hyphenation
Select Tools → Language → Hyphenation.

Manually hyphenate a document
Select Tools → Language → Hyphenation and click the Manual button.

Insert a non-breaking hyphen

Place the insertion point where you want the hyphen and press Ctrl-Shift-Hyphen. A non-breaking hyphen prevents a hyphenated phrase or word from breaking at the end of a line. Instead the entire word or phrase moves to the next line.

Insert an optional hyphen

Place the insertion point where you want the hyphen and press Ctrl-Hyphen. An optional hyphen lets you specify where a word breaks if it comes at the end of a line.

Remove manual hyphenation

Select Edit → Replace and click the More button to reveal additional search options. Next, click the Special button and choose Optional Hyphen. Leave the Replace with box empty and use the Find Next, Replace, or Replace All buttons to search for and remove hyphens.

Exclude a paragraph from automatic hyphenation

Select Format → Paragraph, click the Line and Page Breaks tab, and check the Don't hyphenate box.

Letters, Envelopes, and Labels

Create and print form letters using a list of recipients or an Outlook contact list

In Word 2003, select Tools → Letters and Mailings → Mail Merge (Mail Merge Wizard in Word 2002). Select the Letters option, click the Next link, and follow the steps in the wizard.

In Word 97 and 2000, select Tools → Mail Merge, click the Create button, and choose Form Letters from the drop-down list.

Create and print mailing labels using a list of recipients or an Outlook contact list

In Word 2003, select Tools → Letters and Mailings → Mail Merge (Mail Merge Wizard in Word 2002). Select the Labels option, click the Next link, and follow the steps in the wizard.

In Word 97 and 2000, select Tools → Mail Merge, click the Create button, and choose Mailing Labels from the drop-down list.

02+ *Create and send form email messages using a list of recipients or an Outlook contact list*

Select Tools → Letters and Mailings → Mail Merge (Mail Merge Wizard in Word 2002). Select the E-mail messages option, click the Next link, and follow the steps in the wizard.

02+ *Create and send form faxes using a list of recipients or an Outlook contact list*

Select Tools → Letters and Mailings → Mail Merge (Mail Merge Wizard in Word 2002). Select the Faxes option, click the Next link, and follow the steps in the wizard.

NOTE

The Faxes option is only available during a mail merge if you have a MAPI-compatible fax program and an email program with a fax transport installed.

Create a letter using a wizard

Select Tools → Letters and Mailings → Letter Wizard (Tools → Letter Wizard in Word 97 and 2000).

Print an envelope

Select Tools → Letters and Mailings → Envelopes and Labels (Tools → Envelopes and Labels in Word 97 and 2000) and click the Envelopes tab. Enter a delivery address and return address, and click the Print button.

Use addresses from an address book on an envelope

Select Tools → Letters and Mailings → Envelopes and Labels (Tools → Envelopes and Labels in Word 97 and 2000) and click the Envelopes tab. Next, click the Insert Address icon above the Delivery address box or Return address box to look up an address from your Windows Address Book. (If you highlight an address in a document and then follow these steps, Word pops it into the Delivery address box.)

Change the envelope size and other options

Select Tools → Letters and Mailings → Envelopes and Labels (Tools → Envelopes and Labels in Word 97 and 2000) and click the Envelopes tab. Next, click the Options button and click the Envelope Options tab.

Change how an envelope is printed

Select Tools → Letters and Mailings → Envelopes and Labels (Tools → Envelopes and Labels in Word 97 and 2000) and click the Envelopes tab. Next, click the Options button and click the Printing Options tab.

Print labels

Select Tools → Letters and Mailings → Envelopes and Labels (Tools → Envelopes and Labels in Word 97 and 2000) and click the Labels tab. Enter the address, choose whether to print a single label or a sheet of the same labels, and click the Print button.

Use addresses from an address book for labels

Select Tools → Letters and Mailings → Envelopes and Labels (Tools → Envelopes and Labels in Word 97 and 2000) and click the Labels tab. Next, click the Insert Address icon above the Address box to choose an address from the Windows Address Book.

Select a label type and change label details

Select Tools → Letters and Mailings → Envelopes and Labels (Tools → Envelopes and Labels in Word 97 and 2000), click the Labels tab, and click the Options button.

Setting Other Word Options

This section shows you important, but perhaps lesser known, options available under the Tools menu.

Keep Word from repaginating documents in the background

Select Tools → Options, click the General tab, and uncheck the Background repagination box.

View documents on a blue background with white text

Select Tools → Options, click the General tab, and check the Blue background, white text box.

Use sounds and animated cursors to show what's going on in Word

Select Tools → Options, click the General tab, and check the Provide feedback with sound box and the Provide feedback with animation box.

Have Word ask before converting documents

Select Tools → Options, click the General tab, and check the Confirm conversion at Open box.

Mail documents as attachments instead of in the email message body

Select Tools → Options, click the General tab, and check the Mail as attachment box.

00+ *Set email options when using the File → Send To → Mail Recipient command*

Select Tools → Options, click the General tab, and click the E-Mail Options button.

Change the unit of measurement used in rulers and dialog boxes
> Select Tools → Options, click the General tab, and choose an option from the Measurement units drop-down menu.

00+ *Set options for how Word creates and displays web pages*
> Select Tools → Options, click the General tab, and click the Web Options button.

Change the name, initials, and address you use in Word
> Select Tools → Options and click on the User Information tab.

Pick the substitute font Word uses when you're missing the actual font used in a document
> Select Tools → Options, click on the Compatibility tab, and click the Font Substitution button.

Getting Help

This section shows you how to take advantage of all the help options available in Word, including the Office Assistant, tools for WordPerfect users, and updating and repairing tools.

Make the Office Assistant go away
> In Word 97 and Word 2000, the Office Assistant is installed and displayed by default. Right-click the assistant's icon and choose Hide to temporarily remove the assistant. Right-click the icon and choose Options and uncheck the Use the Office Assistant box to turn it off entirely. (In Word 97, you can't turn off the assistant with one click; you must disable each action it responds to).

View the tips suggested by the Office Assistant
    As you work, a light bulb appears above the Assistant when Word sees an easier way to do something. Click the Assistant to see its suggestions.

Ask Word a question
    Click the Assistant and type a question.

    In Word 2002 and 2003, if the Assistant is turned off, click the Ask a Question box on the menu bar in the upper right corner and type a question.

Use the full help window
    In Word 2000–2003, select Help → Microsoft Word Help or press F1. Click the Content tab to browse topics, the Answer Wizard tab to search for topics, or the Index tab to search for keywords.

    In Word 97, select Help → Contents and Index.

Get a description of a toolbar button or other screen element
    In the main Word window, select Help → What's This? (or press Shift-F1) and then click an interface element (to open a help balloon) or any text (to reveal formatting). This feature is not available in Word 2003.

Get help if you're a WordPerfect user
    Select Help → WordPerfect Help.

Have Word display the equivalent Word command when you press a WordPerfect key combination
    Select Tools → Options, click the General tab, and check the Help for WordPerfect users box.

Change Page Up, Page Down, Home, End, and Esc to their WordPerfect equivalents
    Select Tools → Options, click the General tab, and check the Navigation keys for WordPerfect users box.

00+ *Have Office scan its program files and replace them with the original installation files if any problems are found*

> Select Help → Detect and Repair. You'll need to provide the Office installation CD or the location of the installation files.

Customizing Word

This section shows you how to assign keyboard shortcuts and change the commands on Word's menus and toolbars.

Setting General Customization Options

00+ *Have Word show the full menus instead of only common commands*

> In Word 2002 and 2003, select Tools → Customize, click the Options tab, and check the Always show full menus box.
>
> In Word 2000, select Tools → Customize, click the Options tab, and uncheck the Menus show recently used commands first box.

00+ *Show the Standard toolbar and Formatting toolbar on two rows*

> In Word 2002 and 2003, select Tools → Customize, click the Options tab, and check the Show Standard and Formatting toolbars on two rows box.
>
> In Word 2000, select Tools → Customize, click the Options tab, and uncheck the Standard and Formatting toolbars share one row box.
>
> In Word 2000–2003, you can also drag the Formatting toolbar to the second row to automatically enable this option.

Use larger icons on toolbars

> Select Tools → Customize, click the Options tab, and check the Large icons box.

Specify whether font names should be displayed using the actual font in the Font drop-down list

Select Tools → Customize, click the Options tab, and check the List font names in their font box.

Turn off the pop-up balloon tips showing the names of toolbar buttons

Select Tools → Customize, click the Options tab, and uncheck the Show ScreenTips on toolbars box.

Have Word show shortcut keys for toolbar buttons in pop-up balloon tips

Select Tools → Customize, click the Options tab, and check the Show shortcut keys in ScreenTips box.

Customizing Toolbars and Menus

Turn on toolbars not shown in Word's Toolbars submenu

Select Tools → Customize, click the Toolbars tab, and click the checkbox next to any toolbar to turn it on.

Create a new toolbar that you can fill with buttons and menus

Select Tools → Customize, click the Toolbars tab, and click the New button.

Rename a toolbar that you created

Select Tools → Customize, click the Toolbars tab, select a toolbar, and click the Rename button.

Restore a toolbar to its default settings

Select Tools → Customize, click the Toolbars tab, select a toolbar, and click the Reset button. Then choose whether to reset the toolbar in the open document or the attached template and click the OK button.

Add a command to a toolbar or menu

Select Tools → Customize and click the Commands tab. Select a category and a command. Click the Description button to view a pop-up explanation of the command. Drag the command to any toolbar or menu.

Add a command to a shortcut menu

Select Tools → Customize, click the Toolbars tab, and click the checkbox next to the Shortcut Menus toolbar. Switch to the Commands tab and drag a command to any of the available shortcut menus on the toolbar. The toolbar closes as soon as you close the Customize dialog box. See Part 1 for more on shortcut menus.

Remove a command from a toolbar or menu

Select Tools → Customize and click the Commands tab. Drag the command from the menu and when the icon displays an X, drop the command to remove it.

Without opening the Customize dialog box, hold down the Alt key while dragging any command from the toolbar. (This does not work with menu commands in Word 97, but does work with menus and buttons.)

Change the name of a menu command or toolbar button

Select Tools → Customize. Right-click a command or button and change the value of the Name box on the shortcut menu.

Change the icon used for a command or toolbar button

Select Tools → Customize. Right-click a command or button and choose Change Button Image.

Change how text is displayed for a command or toolbar button

Select Tools → Customize. Right-click a command or button and choose Default Style, Text Only (Always), Text Only (In Menus), or Image and Text.

Insert a dividing line between buttons on a toolbar or commands on a menu

Select Tools → Customize. Right-click a command or button that will be to the right of (or below) the dividing line and choose Begin a Group.

Choose where to save changes made to toolbars and menus

Select Tools → Customize, click the Commands tab, and choose a location from the Save in drop-down menu. The file you specify will be used to save all changes you make while the Customize dialog box is open.

Customizing Keyboard Shortcuts

Find the default keyboard shortcut for a command

Select Tools → Customize and click the Keyboard button. Next, select a category and a command to see current assignments in the Current keys box. Refer to the tables in Part 3 for a list of default keyboard shortcuts.

Assign a keyboard shortcut to a command

Select Tools → Customize and click the Keyboard button. Next, select a category and a command. Click in the Press new shortcut key box and then press the key combination you want to use. Choose where to save the changes and click the Assign button.

Assign a shortcut key to a symbol, special character, font, AutoText entry, macro, or style

Select Tools → Customize and click the Keyboard button. Use the special categories at the bottom of the category list.

> **_Print a list of shortcut keys used in a document or template_**
>
> Select Tools → Macro → Macros. In the Macros in box, select Word commands. In the Macro name box, select ListCommands. Click the Run button. In the List Commands dialog box, select the Current menu and keyboard settings option and click the OK button. A table of shortcut keys is created in the document window.

Collaborating

This section shows you how to use Word's collaboration tools to send and route documents, track changes, insert comments, compare documents, and more.

Sending Documents to People and Places

Send a document by email, making the document the body of the message

Select File → Send To → Mail Recipient.

`00+` _Send a document by email as an attachment_

Select File → Send To → Mail Recipient (as Attachment).

`02+` _Send a document as an attachment for review_

Select File → Send To → Mail Recipient (for Review) to flag the recipient that the document is to be reviewed.

`00+` _Send a document to a folder on an Exchange server or a folder in your Outlook personal folder store_

Select File → Send To → Exchange Folder.

Route a document by email so that multiple people can review it

Select File → Send To → Routing Recipient. You can designate who sees the document and in what sequence, and monitor its progress.

Set compatibility features for users of other versions of Word
Select Tools → Options and click the Compatibility tab. Use the drop-down list, choose the word processing program, and further customize the settings in the Options checkbox list below.

Set a password required to open or modify the document
Select Tools → Options and click the Security tab (select Tools → Options and click the Save tab in Word 97 and 2000). Enter a password and click the OK button. If you forget the password, you'll need to find a third party utility that can crack it. Check out *http://www.elcomsoft.com/* for one such program.

02+ *Have Word suggest that a document be opened as read-only*
Select Tools → Options, click the Security tab, and check the Read-only recommended box.

03+ *Allow only comments or tracked changes in a document you send to someone*
Select Tools → Protect Document and check the Allow only this type of editing in the document box. Choose the restrictions you want and click the Yes, Start Enforcing Protection button.

NOTE

Giving users the right to make tracked changes also gives them the right to insert comments. However, these rights do not let users fill in forms; that right must be given explicitly.

03+ *Protect the formatting of a document you send to someone*
Select Tools → Protect Document and check the Limit formatting to a selection of styles box. Click the Settings link to choose the styles you will allow and click the Yes, Start Enforcing Protection button.

00+ *Start a meeting with someone using NetMeeting and open the current document for review*

Select Tools → Online Collaboration → Meet Now.

Using Shared Workspaces

03+ *Create a shared workspace*

Select Tools → Shared Workspace. Type a workspace name, the URL of a Microsoft Windows SharePoint Services web site that will host the workspace, and click the Create button.

NOTE

Shared workspaces rely on Microsoft Windows SharePoint Services, so you must have a local network server running SharePoint services or have access to one on the Internet. In order to create a workspace, you must also have permission to do so on the chosen web site.

03+ *Create a shared workspace by sending a shared attachment*

In Outlook 2003, create a new email message and address it to the recipients with whom you want to share the document. Click Insert → File, locate the document, and click the Insert button. In the Attachment Options task pane (click Attachment Options on the toolbar if the pane is not visible), click Shared Attachments and fill in the URL of the SharePoint Services web site.

03+ *Add members to a shared workspace*

Select Tools → Shared Workspace, click the Members tab, and click the Add New Members link.

03+ *Delete a shared workspace*

Select Tools → Shared Workspace, click the down arrow that appears when you hold your pointer over the title of the shared workspace, and then select Delete Workspace from the pop-up menu. Note that you must be an administrator of a workspace in order to delete it.

13+ *Make Word stop asking if you want to update shared documents*

Select Tools → Shared Workspace, click the down arrow that appears when you hold your pointer over the title of the document, and then select Disconnect from Workspace from the pop-up menu. The document is no longer associated with the workspace.

If you want to reconnect to the workspace and share the document again, you must first recreate the shared workspace. Once that's done, switch to the Status tab and click the Document Updates link. Note that your copy will replace the shared workspace copy and other people sharing the workspace may be asked to resolve any conflicts that arise.

Comments

View comments

In Word 2002 and 2003, click the Reviewing Pane button on the Reviewing toolbar.

In Word 97 and 2000, select View → Comments.

Insert a new comment

Place the insertion point or make a selection and choose Insert → Comment or click the Insert Comment button (New Comment button in Word 2002) on the Reviewing toolbar.

Edit a comment

In Word 2002 and 2003, click the text of a comment in the Reviewing Pane (or balloon in Print Layout view) and make your changes.

In Word 97 and 2000, select View → Comments, click the relevant text in the Comment pane, and make your changes.

Delete a comment

In Word 2002 and 2003, right-click the comment in the main text, comment bubble (Print Layout view), or

Reviewing Pane, and select Delete Comment. You can also select the comment and click the Reject Change/Delete Comment button on the Reviewing toolbar.

In Word 97 and 2000, right-click the comment in the main document and select Delete Comment.

02+ *Delete all comments*

On the Reviewing toolbar, click the down arrow next to the Reject Change/Delete Comment button and choose Delete All Comments in Document.

03+ *Delete all ink annotations*

On the Reviewing toolbar, click the down arrow next to the Reject Change/Delete Comment button and choose Delete All Ink Annotations in Document.

02+ *Change the format used for comment text in comment bubbles*

Select View → Print Layout and click in a comment bubble (not the reviewing pane). Select Format → Styles and Formatting, click the down arrow in the Comment Text box, and choose Modify.

Tracking Changes

Hide or show all tracked changes in a document

In Word 2002 and 2003, select View → Markup.

In Word 97 and 2000, select Tools → Track Changes → Highlight Changes. Check the Highlight changes on screen box and click the OK button.

Have Word track the changes to a document

In Word 2002 and 2003, select Tools → Track Changes, press Ctrl-Shift-E, or double-click the TRK button on the status bar to turn tracking on or off.

In Word 97 and 2000, select Tools → Track Changes → Highlight Changes and check the Track changes while editing box. You can also press Ctrl-Shift-E, or double-click the TRK button on the status bar to turn tracking on or off.

Choose the specific markup types to display

On the Reviewing toolbar, click the Show menu to hide or show changes by the type of change or by reviewer.

Change how tracked changes are displayed

In Word 2002 and 2003, make a selection from the Display for Review drop-down list on the Reviewing toolbar.

In Word 97 and 2000, select Tools → Track Changes → Highlight Changes.

Move between changes in a document

In Word 2002 and 2003, click the Previous or Next button on the Reviewing toolbar. In Word 97 and 2000, click the Previous Change or Next Change button on the Reviewing toolbar.

Make a change permanent

On the Reviewing toolbar, click the Accept Change button.

Or right-click a change in the document window and choose Accept Change (the command changes in Word 2002 and 2003 depending on the type of change).

You can also select a range of text and accept all the changes in it using the Accept Change button.

Accept all changes in a document

In Word 2002 and 2003, click the down arrow next to the Accept Change button on the Reviewing toolbar and choose Accept All Changes in Document.

In Word 97 and 2000, select Tools → Track Changes → Accept or Reject Changes and click the Accept All button.

Undo a change

On the Reviewing toolbar, click the Reject Change/ Delete Comment button (the Reject Change button in Word 97 and 2000).

Or right-click a change in the document window and choose Reject Change (the command changes in Word 2002 and 2003 depending on the type of change).

Select a range of text and click the Reject Change/Delete Comment button (the Reject Change button in Word 97 and 2000) to reject all changes in the text.

Reject all changes in a document

In Word 2002 and 2003, click the down arrow next to the Reject Change/Delete Comment button on the Reviewing toolbar and choose Reject All Changes in Document.

In Word 97 and 2000, select Tools → Track Changes → Accept or Reject Changes and click the Reject All button.

Change basic options for tracking changes

In Word 2002 and 2003, select Tools → Options and click the Track Changes tab or click the Show button on the Reviewing toolbar and choose Options.

In Word 97 and 2000, select Tools → Track Changes → Highlight Changes and click the Options button.

In all versions, right-click the TRK button in the status bar and select Options.

02+ *Change whether markup balloons are used in Print and Web Layout views*

In Word 2003, select Tools → Options, click the Track Changes tab, and choose an option from the Use Balloons (Print and Web Layout) drop-down menu.

In Word 2002, select Tools → Options, click the Track Changes tab, and check the Use Balloons in Print and Web Layout box.

02+ *Change the size and placement of markup balloons*

Select Tools → Options, click the Track Changes tab, and use the options in the Balloons section of the dialog box.

Change how Word uses vertical lines in the margin to indicate changes

In Word 2002 and 2003, select Tools → Options, click the Track Changes tab, and use the options in the Changed Lines section of the dialog box.

In Word 97 and 2000, select Tools → Track Changes → Highlight Changes and click the Options button.

02+

Print the markup in a document

Select File → Print and choose either Document showing markup or List of markup from the Print what drop-down list.

Protect the changes or comments in a document when sending it for review

Select Tools → Protect Document and choose Tracked changes to prevent a user from turning off tracked changes and from accepting or rejecting changes. Specify a password to prevent other users from removing protection via the same method.

Comparing Documents

Compare and merge two documents and view the differences using tracked changes

In Word 2002 and 2003, open one document (preferably an edited copy). Select Tools → Compare and Merge Documents. Select the second document (preferably the original copy), and then choose one of the following options:

- To display results as marked changes in the second document (the original), click the Merge button.
- To display results as marked changes in the first document (the copy), choose Merge into current document from the Merge button's drop-down list.
- To display results as marked changes in a new document, choose Merge into new document from the Merge button's drop-down list.

In Word 97 and 2000, open one document and select Tools → Merge Documents to select another document to merge into the first.

Use the Compare and Merge feature on two or more documents

You can repeat the Tools → Compare and Merge Documents (Tools → Merge Documents in Word 97 and 2000) process on multiple documents. This works fairly well for bringing in small changes from multiple reviewers. However, it's usually easier to merge two documents, go through the changes, and then merge additional documents one at a time.

02+ *Compare document using a legal black line instead of tracked changes*

Open the first document, choose Tools → Compare and Merge Documents, check the Legal blackline box, select the second document, and click the Compare button. A third document is created, showing only what changed between the two documents.

03+ *Compare two documents side-by-side*

First, open both documents. While viewing either document, select Window → Compare Side by Side with *filename*, where *filename* is the name of the other document. (If you have more than two documents open, the Compare Side by Side with command opens a dialog box that lets you choose one of the open documents for comparison.) Both documents are shown side-by-side. Scrolling is synchronized to make comparison easier. A Compare Side by Side toolbar lets you disable synchronized scrolling, reset the view, and close the side-by-side comparison.

Use web discussions for a document

Select Tools → Online Collaboration → Web Discussions. Web discussions are shown in a separate pane at the bottom of the document and a Web Discussions toolbar opens with options for creating, replying to, filtering,

---

and printing discussions. This feature requires that a discussion server be set up and configured on your network. The first time you use the feature, you may be prompted to select a discussion server.

NOTE

Web discussions are server-based additions that work much like Word's commenting feature, except that they let multiple reviewers participate in a discussion regardless of which version they possess. The new, shared workspace features of Word 2003 have largely supplanted web discussions.

Using Macros

A macro lets you perform a set of tasks or steps in Word using a single keystroke. This section describes the basics of using macros in Word.

Record a new macro
    Select Tools → Macro → Record New Macro. Name the macro, choose where to assign and save it, click the OK button, and perform the actions you want to record. Use the record, pause, and stop buttons on the Stop Recording toolbar to control the recording.

Run a macro
    Select Tools → Macro → Macros (or press Alt-F8).

Delete a macro
    Select Tools → Macro → Macros, select the macro, and click the Delete button.

Copy macros to another document or template
    Select Tools → Macro → Macros and click the Organizer button.

    Select Tools → Templates and Add-Ins, click the Organizer button, and click the Macro Project Items tab.

> **Set a security level for running macros when a document opens**
>
> In Word 2000-2003, select Tools → Macro → Security and click the Security Level tab. Choose a security level (High, Medium, or Low) and click the OK button.
>
> In Word 97, select Tools → Options, click the General tab, and check the Macro virus protection box. Enabling this option forces Word to prompt you when opening a document with macros.

00+ *View trusted sources for macros*

Select Tools → Macro → Security and click the Trusted Publishers tab (Trusted Sources tab in Word 2000 and 2002).

Run a macro one step at a time, showing me each step in VBA as it occurs in Word

Select Tools → Macro → Macros, select the macro, and click the Step Into button.

Launch Visual Basic for Applications to create or edit a macro

Select Tools → Macro → Visual Basic Editor (or press Alt-F11).

PART III

Word Reference

This part of the book provides reference information that's often hard to find or missing from the manual, including:

- Useful commands not included on any toolbar or menu by default (Table 2)
- Text and graphic file formats natively supported by Word (Tables 3 and 4)
- Switches to start Word from the command line or Start ▸ Run dialog (Table 5)
- Wildcards and character codes for search-and-replace operations (Tables 6 and 7)
- Locations of important Word files and default paths for saving files (Table 8)

In addition, this part lists default key combinations (keyboard shortcuts) for:

- Selecting, formatting, and editing text (Tables 9–15)
- Inserting and reviewing text (Tables 16 and 17)
- Performing a mail merge (Table 18)
- Printing and previewing (Table 19)
- Fields (Table 20)
- Outlines (Table 21)
- Command bars (Table 22)
- Windows and dialog boxes (Table 23)
- The Web (Table 24)

- Cross-references and footnotes (Table 25)
- Office Assistant keys (Table 26)
- Task Pane keys (Table 27)

To assign your own keyboard shortcuts for many of these and other Word operations, select Tools → Customize and click the Keyboard button.

Command Reference

There are over 1,000 commands available in Word 2003 and only some of them make their way onto Word's menus and toolbars or were given keyboard shortcuts. Table 2 lists some useful commands and suggestions on where you might add them. To see all the commands built into Word, select Tools → Customize, click the Commands tab, and select All Commands from the Categories list. Check out the section on customizing Word in Part 2 for details on adding these commands to the interface.

Table 2. Useful Word commands

Command	Action	Suggested uses
ResetChar	Removes all character formatting, reverting text to the default paragraph formatting. Same as pressing Ctrl-Space or choosing Clear Formatting from Style drop-down menu.	Add button to Formatting toolbar, Text shortcut menu, or create as macro.
Hidden	Applies the Hidden format to selected text, same as if you choose Format → Font and select the Hidden option.	Add to shortcut menu or toolbar for hiding text within a document. See Part 2 for more.
NextMisspelling	Jumps to the next misspelled word, selects it, and opens a shortcut menu.	Add to a toolbar to quickly browse through misspelled words in a document.

Table 2. Useful Word commands (continued)

Command	Action	Suggested uses
AutoScroll	Automatically scrolls the document in the direction that you move the mouse. Some three-button mice do this when you click the middle button.	Add to a toolbar to easily scan through long documents.
ApplyHeadingX	Three commands (ApplyHeading1–3) apply the default heading paragraph styles. Same as Alt-Ctrl-*x* (where *x* is the heading number).	Add to the Text shortcut menu to quickly create or change headings throughout a document.
EditSwapAllNotes	Changes all footnotes in a document to endnotes and vice versa.	Add to a toolbar for quick conversion without having to select and convert individual notes.
EndOfWindowExtend	Extend the current selection (or create a new selection from the insertion point) to the last line fully displayed in the document window.	Add to a toolbar or shortcut menu, or create a keyboard shortcut to extend your selection capabilities.
MenuWork	A new menu that works like a favorites menu for Word documents. You can add any document you like to the menu for quick access.	Add to Word's menu bar.
SentLeft (SentRight)	Moves the insertion point to the beginning of the previous (sentleft) or next (sentright) sentence.	Add to toolbar or create a keyboard shortcut for browsing sentences.
SentLeftExtend (SentRightExtend)	Extends the selection to include the previous or next sentence.	Add to toolbar or shortcut menu or create a keyboard shortcut.
SkipNumbering	Removes numbering or bullets from the selected paragraphs and continues the numbering or bulleting for subsequent items.	Add to toolbar or Lists shortcut menu.

Table 2. Useful Word commands (continued)

Command	Action	Suggested uses
TableSelectTable	Selects an entire table. Pressing Alt-5 (using the 5 on the number pad) while NumLock is turned off also selects a table.	Add to Table Cell, Table Text, and Table Lists shortcut menus.
ToolsCustomizeKey-Board	Opens the Customize Keyboard dialog (Tools → Customize → Keyboard).	Add to a toolbar for quick access.
ToolsCustomizeKey-BoardShortcut	Changes the pointer to a command button. Click any toolbar button or menu command to open the Customize Keyboard dialog box with that command selected.	Add to a toolbar to quickly customize any command.
ToolsSpellingHide	Hides/shows the squiggly red lines under misspelled words.	Add to toolbar for quick access.
ToolsGrammarHide	Hides/shows the squiggly green lines under grammatical errors.	Add to toolbar for quick access.

Native Formats

Word 2003 supports many text and graphic formats (with no conversion required). Table 3 lists all the text formats native to Word 2003. Table 4 shows the native graphics formats.

NOTE

Word can use other text and graphics formats if you installed the correct filters, some of which are included with the Word installation files. You can install these filters during the initial installation of Word or by inserting the installation CD later and using the Add or Remove features option.

Table 3. Native text formats Word can open and save

Format	File extension
Word 2003, 2002, Word 2000, and Word 97 for Windows	*.doc*
Word 98 for Macintosh	*.doc*
XML	*.xml*
HTML	*.htm* and *.html*
MS-DOS Text	*.txt*
MS-DOS Text with Line Breaks	*.txt*
Rich Text Format	*.rtf*
Text Only	*.txt*
Text with Line Breaks	*.txt*
Unicode Text	*.txt*
Word 6.0/95 for Windows & Macintosh	*.doc*
Word 4.x–5.1 for Macintosh (open only)	*.mcw*
Word 2.0 and 1.0 for Windows (open only)	*.doc*

Table 4. Native graphic formats

Format	File extension	Versions	Notes
Graphics Interchange Format	*.gif*	Native in Word 2000, 2002, and 2003. Word 97 imports using HTML converter.	Supports versions GIF87a (including interlacing) and GIF89a (including interlacing and transparency).
Joint Photographic Experts Group	*.jpg* *.jpeg*	Native in all versions.	Supports version 6.0 of the JPEG File Interchange Format (JFIF).
Portable Network Graphics	*.png*	Native in all versions.	Supports files conforming to the Tenth Specification Version 1.0.
Windows bitmap	*.bmp*	Native in all versions.	Supports Windows and OS/2 bitmaps, Run Length Encoded (RLE) bitmaps, and device-independent bitmaps (DIB).

Table 4. Native graphic formats (continued)

Format	File extension	Versions	Notes
Tagged Image File Format	*.tiff*	Native in Word 2000, 2002, and 2003. Word 97 converts on opening.	Supports TIFF Specification Revision 5.0 and 6.0, Part1: Baseline TIFF.
Windows Enhanced Metafile	*.emf*	Native in all versions.	
Windows Metafile	*.wmf*	Native in all versions.	

Startup Switches

As with most programs, you can start Word from the Windows command line (Start → Programs → MS-DOS Prompt in Windows 95 and 98, Start → Programs → Accessories → MS-DOS Prompt in Me, and Start → Programs → Accessories → Command Prompt in Windows 2000/XP), the Start → Run dialog in all Windows versions, or a customized shortcut. At the prompt, type winword.exe to launch Word normally, or add one of the switches listed in Table 5 after the command to affect how Word launches (for instance, winword.exe /n).

Table 5. Command-line startup switches

Startup switch	Description
filename	Starts Word and opens the specified file. You can specify more than one filename (separated by spaces) to open multiple documents.
/a	Starts Word and prevents add-ins and global templates from loading. The switch also locks Word's setting files so you can't modify them.
/c	Starts Word and then starts NetMeeting.

Table 5. Command-line startup switches (continued)

Startup switch	Description
/l addinpath	Starts Word normally and loads a specific add in or global template. For example, winword.exe /l c:\ word\ newglobal.dot loads a template named *newglobal.dot* found in the *C:\word* folder.
/m	Starts Word without running any AutoExec macros that execute when the program loads or a specific document opens. Alternate method: hold down the Shift key and start Word normally.
/mfile *n*	Starts Word and opens the file in the specified (*n*) position on the Most Recently Used file list on the File menu.
/m macroname	Starts Word and runs the specified macro; AutoExec macros are disabled.
/n	Starts a new instance of Word with no document open. Documents opened in each instance of Word will not appear as choices in the Window menu of other instances.
/w	Starts a new instance of Word with a blank document. Documents opened in each instance of Word will not appear as choices in the Window menu of the other instances.
/q	Starts Word without displaying the splash screen (Word 2000 and later).
/t template_ name	Starts Word with a new document based on a template other than *Normal.dot*.
/r	Starts Word in the background, re-registers Word and its file type associations in the Windows Registry. Use if you are having problems with file type associations.

Wildcards and Find Codes

You can do sophisticated searches using the Edit → Find and Edit → Replace commands in combination with wildcards and special character codes. In order to use wildcards, in the Find and Replace dialog, click the More button to reveal additional search options, and check the Use wildcards box. Note that many of the special character codes work differently when the Use wildcards option is turned on or off.

NOTE

Table 6 lists Wildcards and Table 7 lists special character codes. In the world outside Word, *wildcards* are known as *regular expressions*, and are a special syntax for handling text. Technically, wildcards are only a subset of regular expressions (such as the ? and * symbols), though Microsoft has decided to refer to all regular expressions as wildcards in Word. They work a little differently (as do most implementations of regular expressions), but achieve much the same effect.

Table 6. Wildcards used in the Find and Replace dialog

Name	Symbol	Example
Any character	?	"a?t" finds "act" and "art"
Specified characters	[ ]	"[fp]act" finds "fact" and "pact"
Any character in range	[-]	"[a-o]act" finds "fact" but not "pact"
Any character not in range	[! -]	"[!a-o]act" finds "pact" but not "fact"
Beginning of word	<	"<act" finds "act" and "action"
End of word	>	">act" finds "react" and "fact"
Not	[!]	"[!p]act" finds "act" and "fact" but not "pact"
0 or more characters	*	"*act>" finds all words where "act" are the last three letters.
Exactly *n* occurrences of a character	{n}	"re{2}d" finds all occurrences of "reed" but not "red"
At least *n* occurrences of a character	{n,}	"re{1,}d" finds all occurrences of "reed" and "red"
Between *n* and *m* occurrences of a character	{n,m}	"15{1-3}" finds "150", "1500", and "15000", but not "150,000"
One or more occurrences of the previous character	@	"re@d" finds "red", "reed", and "readiness"

Table 7. Character codes in the Find and Replace dialog

Special Character	Symbol	Notes
Paragraph mark	^p	Cannot be used in the Find what box when wildcard search is enabled. With Wildcards on, use ^13 in the Find what box instead.
Tab	^t	
ANSI or ASCII characters	^0nnn	*nnn* represents the character code. For example, type ^0114 to find the letter "r."
Em dash	^+	
En dash	^=	
Caret character	^^	
Manual line break	^l	
Column break	^n	
Manual page break	^m	Searches for section breaks when wildcards are turned on.
Nonbreaking space	^s	
Nonbreaking hyphen	^~	
Optional hyphen	^-	
Graphic	^g	Works only with Find (not Replace). Wildcards must be turned on.
Any character	^?	Works only with Find. Wildcards must be turned off.
Any digit	^#	Works only with Find. Wildcards must be turned off.
Any letter	^$	Works only with Find. Wildcards must be turned off.
Footnote mark	^f	Works only with Find. Wildcards must be turned off. With wildcards on, use ^2 instead.
Endnote mark	^e	Works only with Find. Wildcards must be turned off.
Field	^d	Works only with Find. Wildcards must be turned off. With wildcards turned on, use ^19 instead.
Section break	^b	Works only with Find. Wildcards must be turned off.

Table 7. Character codes in the Find and Replace dialog (continued)

Special Character	Symbol	Notes
White space (regular and nonbreaking spaces and tabs)	^w	Works only with Find. Wildcards must be turned off.
Windows Clipboard contents	^c	Works only with Replace (not Find).
Contents of the Find what box	^&	Works only with Replace (not Find).

Default File Locations

Table 8 lists the locations of important files and folders for the most recent versions of Word. Some of these locations are user-definable; some are not. As you scan the tables, please keep in mind that Word 2003 only runs on Windows 2000 (Service Pack 3 or later) and Windows XP.

Table 8. Default file locations

File or location	Operating system	Path	User-definable
Document storage	Windows 95/98/Me	C:\My Documents	Yes
	Windows 2000/XP	C:\Documents and Settings\ <username>\ My Documents	Yes
User Templates (including *Normal.dot*)	Word 2000 and 2002 in Windows 95/98/ Me	C:\Windows\ Application Data\ Microsoft\ Templates	Yes
	Word 2000, 2002, and 2003 in Windows 2000/XP	C:\Documents and Settings\ <username>\ Application Data\ Microsoft\Templates	Yes
	Word 97 in Windows 95-XP	C:\Program Files\ Microsoft Office\ Templates	Yes

Table 8. Default file locations (continued)

File or location	Operating system	Path	User-definable
Workgroup Templates		No default directory. Select Tools → Options and click on the File Locations tab to set a directory.	Yes
AutoRecover Files	Windows 95/98/Me	C:\Windows\ Application Data\ Microsoft\Word	Yes
	Windows 2000/XP	C:\Documents and Settings\username\ Application Data\ Microsoft\Word	Yes
Startup directory for additional templates or add-ins	Word 2000 and 2002 in Windows 95/98/ Me	C:\Windows\ Application Data\ Microsoft\Word\ Startup	Yes
	Word 2000, 2002, and 2003 in Windows 2000/XP	C:\Documents and Settings\ <username>\ Application Data\ Microsoft\Word\ Startup	Yes
	Word 97 in Windows 95–XP	C:\Program Files\ Microsoft Office\ Office\ Startup	Yes
Built-in templates and wizards (English-language installation)	Windows 95–XP	C:\Program Files\ Microsoft Office\ Templates\1033	No
Program Files	Word 2003 in Windows 2000 SP3, XP	C:\Program Files\ Microsoft Office\ Office11	Only at installation
	Word 2002 in Windows 2000 SP3, XP	C:\Program Files\ Microsoft Office\ Office10	Only at installation

Table 8. Default file locations (continued)

File or location	Operating system	Path	User-definable
	Word 97 and 2000 in Windows 95–XP	C:\Program Files\ Microsoft Office\ Office	Only at installation
Startup folder for all users	Windows 95–XP	C:\Program Files\ Microsoft Office\ Office10\Startup	No
History of recently opened documents	Windows 95/98/Me	C:\Windows\ Application Data\ Microsoft\Office\ Recent	No
	Windows 2000/XP	C:\Documents and Settings\ <username>\ Application Data\ Microsoft\Office\ Recent	No

Keyboard Shortcuts

Word has hundreds of built-in key combinations. But don't be overwhelmed: start with a handful that represent frequent tasks you perform.

NOTE

Word also lets you assign your own key combinations, as described in Part 2, *Word Tasks*. Key combinations you assign override any built-in combinations using the same keystrokes.

The following tables of default key combinations (Tables 9–27) are grouped by function, such as selecting text, applying character formatting, or working with tables. Unless otherwise noted, these shortcuts work the same in Word 97, 2000, 2002, and 2003.

Table 9. General program keys

Key	Action
Ctrl-N	Create a new document
Ctrl-O or Ctrl-F12	Open a document
Ctrl-S or Shift-F12	Save a document
F12	Open the Save As dialog box
Ctrl-W, Ctrl-F4, or Alt-F4	Close a document. (If only one document is open, Alt-F4 also exits Word.)
Ctrl-Z	Undo an action
Ctrl-Y or F4	Redo or repeat an action
Alt-Ctrl-S	Split a document or remove a split view
Alt-Ctrl-P	Switch to page layout view
Alt-Ctrl-O	Switch to outline view
Alt-Ctrl-N	Switch to normal view
Alt-R	Switch to reading view (Word 2003 only)
Ctrl-\	Move between a master document and its subdocuments
F1	Open Help or Office Assistant
Shift-F1	Context-sensitive help or reveal formatting (same as Help → What's This? in Word 97–2002)
Ctrl-F6	Go to the next Window
Ctrl-Shift-F6	Go to the previous window
F6	In Word 2002 and 2003, switch between the Help task pane and Word
F7	Run the Spelling and Grammar checker
Shift-F7	Open the thesaurus
F10 or Alt	Activate the Menu bar
Ctrl-Tab and Ctrl-Shift-Tab	Cycles through menu and toolbars (and the task pane, if it is open) after pressing F10 or Alt to activate the menu bar

Table 9. General program keys (continued)

Key	Action
Shift-F10 or the context button on some keyboards	Open a context menu

Table 10. Movement keys

Key	Action
Left arrow	Move the insertion point one character to the left
Right arrow	Move one character to the right
Ctrl-Left arrow	Move one word to the left
Ctrl-Right arrow	Move one word to the right
Ctrl-Up arrow	Move one paragraph up
Ctrl-Down arrow	Move one paragraph down
Up arrow	Move up one line
Down arrow	Move down one line
End	Move to the end of a line
Home	Move to the beginning of a line
Alt-Ctrl-Page Up	Move to the top of the window
Alt-Ctrl-Page Down	Move to the end of the window
Page Up	Move up one screen
Page Down	Move down one screen
Ctrl-Page Up	Move to the previous browse object
Ctrl-Page Down	Move to the next browse object
Ctrl-Home	Move to the beginning of a document
Ctrl-End	Move to the end of a document

Table 10. Movement keys (continued)

Key	Action
Shift-F5	Cycle through the last three locations where the insertion point was placed. If you've just opened a document, Shift-F5 returns you to the location you were editing before you closed the document.

Table 11. Selection keys

Key	Action
Shift-Right arrow	Extend selection one character to the right
Shift-Left arrow	Extend selection one character to the left
Ctrl-Shift-Right arrow	Extend selection to the end of the next word
Ctrl-Shift-Left arrow	Extend selection to the beginning of the previous word
Shift-End	Extend selection to the end of a line
Shift-Home	Extend selection to the beginning of a line
Shift-Down arrow	Extend selection one line down
Shift-Up arrow	Extend selection one line up
Ctrl-Shift-Down arrow	Extend selection to the end of a paragraph
Ctrl-Shift-Up arrow	Extend selection to the beginning of a paragraph
Shift-Page Down	Extend selection one screen down
Shift-Page Up	Extend selection one screen up
Ctrl-Shift-Home	Extend selection to the beginning of a document
Ctrl-Shift-End	Extend selection to the end of a document
Ctrl-A	Select the entire document

Table 11. Selection keys (continued)

Key	Action
F8	Enter extend selection mode. Use the arrow keys to extend selection. Press F8 repeatedly to extend a selection as follows: first enters mode, second selects word next to insertion point, third selects the whole sentence, fourth selects all characters in paragraph (including the paragraph mark), fifth adds the whole document. Press Shift-F8 to reduce the size of a selection. Press ESC to exit mode.
Ctrl-Shift-F8	Select a column of text. Once a column is selected, use the arrow keys to extend the selection one column at a time.

Table 12. Character formatting keys

Key	Action
Ctrl-Shift-F	Activate the Font drop-down menu on the Formatting toolbar
Ctrl-Shift-P	Activate the Font Size drop-down menu on the Formatting toolbar
Ctrl-Shift->	Increase the font size according to the preset sizes
Ctrl-Shift-<	Decrease the font size according to the preset sizes
Ctrl-]	Increase the font size by 1 point
Ctrl-[	Decrease the font size by 1 point
Ctrl-D	Open the Font dialog box
Shift-F3	Cycle through the available case formats for letters
Ctrl-Shift-A	Format letters as all capitals
Ctrl-Shift-K	Format letters as small capitals
Ctrl-B	Apply bold formatting
Ctrl-I	Apply italic formatting
Ctrl-U	Apply underline formatting
Ctrl-Shift-W	Underline words but not spaces
Ctrl-Shift-D	Double-underline text
Ctrl-Shift-H	Apply hidden text formatting
Ctrl-=	Apply subscript formatting (automatic spacing)
Ctrl-Shift-+	Apply superscript formatting (automatic spacing)
Ctrl-Shift-Q	Change the selection to Symbol font

Table 12. Character formatting keys (continued)

Key	Action
Ctrl-Shift-*	Display non-printing characters
Ctrl-Shift-C	Copy formats
Ctrl-Shift-V	Paste formats
Shift-F1	Review text formatting (same as Help → What's This? In Word 97–2002)
Ctrl-Spacebar	Remove manual character formatting

Table 13. Paragraph formatting keys

Key	Action
Ctrl-1	Single-space lines
Ctrl-2	Double-space lines
Ctrl-5	Set 1.5-line spacing
Ctrl-0 (zero)	Add/Remove one-line spacing preceding a paragraph
Ctrl-E	Center a paragraph
Ctrl-J	Justify a paragraph
Ctrl-L	Left-align a paragraph
Ctrl-R	Right-align a paragraph
Ctrl-M	Indent a paragraph from the left
Ctrl-Shift-M	Remove a paragraph indent from the left
Ctrl-T	Create a hanging indent
Ctrl-Shift-T	Reduce a hanging indent
Ctrl-Shift-S	Activate the Style drop-down list on the Formatting toolbar
Alt-Ctrl-K	Start AutoFormat
Ctrl-Shift-N	Apply the Normal style
Alt-Ctrl-1	Apply the Heading 1 style
Alt-Ctrl-2	Apply the Heading 2 style
Alt-Ctrl-3	Apply the Heading 3 style
Ctrl-Shift-L	Apply the List style
Ctrl-Q	Remove paragraph formatting

Table 14. Editing keys

Key	Action
Backspace	Delete one character to the left
Ctrl-Backspace	Delete one word to the left
Delete	Delete one character to the right
Ctrl-Delete	Delete one word to the right
Ctrl-X or Shift-Delete	Cut selected text or graphics to the Clipboard
Ctrl-F3	Cut selected text to the Spike
Ctrl-C or Ctrl-Insert	Copy text or graphics to the Clipboard
Ctrl-V or Shift-Insert	Paste the Clipboard contents
Ctrl-Shift-F3	Paste the Spike contents
Press Ctrl-C twice	Display the Clipboard
F2	To move selected text or graphics, press F2, move the insertion point, and then press Enter
Alt-F3	Create AutoText
Alt-Shift-R	Copy the header or footer used in the previous section of the document

Table 15. Insertion keys

Key	Action
Ctrl-F9	Insert an empty field
Shift-Enter	Insert a line break
Ctrl-Enter	Insert a page break
Ctrl-Shift-Enter	Insert a column break
Ctrl- - (hyphen)	Insert an optional hyphen
Ctrl-Shift- - (hyphen)	Insert a non-breaking hyphen

Table 15. Insertion keys (continued)

Key	Action
Ctrl-Shift-Spacebar	Insert a non-breaking space
Alt-Ctrl-C	Insert a copyright symbol
Alt-Ctrl-R	Insert a registered trademark symbol
Alt-Ctrl-T	Insert a trademark symbol
Alt-Ctrl-. (period)	Insert an ellipsis
Ctrl- - (minus sign)	Insert an en dash
Alt-Ctrl- - (minus sign)	Insert an em dash
Alt-Ctrl-E	In Word 2000–2003, insert a Euro symbol. In Word 97, this shortcut opens the endnote pane.

Table 16. Table keys

Key	Action
Tab	Move to the next cell in a row and select its contents, if any
Shift-Tab	Move to and select the previous cell in a row
Alt-Home	Move to the first cell in a row
Alt-End	Move to the last cell in a row
Alt-Page Up	Move to the first cell in a column
Alt-Page Down	Move to the last cell in a column
Up arrow	Move to the previous row
Down arrow	Move to the next row
Shift-Up arrow	Select the cell in the previous row. Continue pressing the arrow key while the Shift key is depressed to add more rows to the selection.
Alt-5 on keypad (with Num Lock off)	Select an entire table

Table 17. Reviewing keys

Key	Action
Alt-Ctrl-M	Insert a comment
Ctrl-Shift-E	Turn revision marks on or off
Ctrl-Home	Go to the beginning of a comment
Ctrl-End	Go to the end of a comment

Table 18. Mail merge keys

Key	Action
Alt-Shift-K	Preview a mail merge
Alt-Shift-N	Merge a document
Alt-Shift-M	Print the merged document
Alt-Shift-E	Edit a mail-merge data document
Alt-Shift-F	Insert a merge field

Table 19. Printing and previewing keys

Key	Action
Ctrl-P	Print a document
Alt-Ctrl-I	Switch to Print Preview (Press ESC to return to normal view.)
Arrow keys	Move around the preview page when zoomed in
Page Up or Page Down	Move by one preview page when zoomed out
Ctrl-Home	Move to the first preview page when zoomed out
Ctrl-End	Move to the last preview page when zoomed out

Table 20. Field keys

Key	Action
Alt-Shift-D	Insert a DATE field
Alt-Shift-P	Insert a PAGE field
Alt-Shift-T	Insert a TIME field

Table 20. Field keys (continued)

Key	Action
Alt-Ctrl-L	In Word 97, insert a LISTNUM field. In Word 2000–2003, Alt- Ctrl-L makes a line part of a numbered list (you must use the keystroke at the beginning of each line of the list).
Ctrl-F9	Insert an empty field and move the insertion point inside it
F9	Update selected fields
Shift-F9	Toggle display of field codes for whole document
Ctrl-Shift-F9	Unlink a field
F11	Go to next field
Shift-F11	Go to previous field
Ctrl-F11	Lock selected field
Ctrl-Shift-F11	Unlock selected field

Table 21. Outlining keys

Key	Action
Alt-Shift-Left arrow	Promote a paragraph
Alt-Shift-Right arrow	Demote a paragraph
Ctrl-Shift-N	Demote a heading to body text
Alt-Shift-Up arrow	Move selected paragraphs up
Alt-Shift-Down arrow	Move selected paragraphs down
Alt-Shift-+	Expand text under a heading
Alt-Shift- - (minus sign)	Collapse text under a heading
Alt-Shift-A or just the asterisk (*) key on the numeric keypad	Expand or collapse all text or headings
Slash (/) key on the numeric keypad	Hide or display character formatting
Alt-Shift-L	Show the first line of body text or all body text
Alt-Shift-1	Show all headings with the Heading 1 style
Alt-Shift-*n*	Show all headings up to Heading n

Table 22. Command bar keys

Key	Action
Shift-F10	Open a context menu
F10 or Alt	Make the menu bar active or close an active menu. With the menu bar active, press the underlined letter of a menu or command to activate it.
Ctrl-Tab	Move to the next toolbar or menu bar
Ctrl-Shift-Tab	Move to the previous toolbar or menu bar
Arrow keys	Move between commands on an active menu bar
Enter	Activate a selected command
Home	Select the first command on an active menu or submenu
End	Select the last command on an active menu or submenu
Esc	Close a visible menu or submenu, leaving the menu bar active
Ctrl-Alt- - (hyphen)	Pointer turns to minus sign. Open menu and click a command to remove from the menu.

Table 23. Common Windows and dialog box keys

Key	Action
Alt-Tab	Switch to the next program
Alt-Shift-Tab	Switch to the previous program
Ctrl-Esc or Windows logo key	Show the Windows Start menu
Ctrl-W	Close the active document window
Ctrl-F10	Maximize or Restore the document window
Ctrl-F5	Restore the active document window (same as clicking the Restore Down button on a window)
Ctrl-F6	Switch to the next document window
Ctrl-Shift-F6	Switch to the previous document window
Alt-I	Open the folder list in the Open or Save As dialog box. Use the up and down arrow keys to select a folder from the list.

Table 23. Common Windows and dialog box keys (continued)

Key	Action
Alt-O (zero)	Move the focus to the file list in the Open or Save As dialog box. Use the up and down arrows to select a file.
Alt-O or Enter	Open the selected file in the Open or Save As dialog box. Same as clicking Open button.
F5	Update (refresh) the files visible in the Open or Save As dialog box
Ctrl-Tab	Switch to the next tab in a dialog box
Ctrl-Shift-Tab	Switch to the previous tab in a dialog box
Tab	Move to the next option on a dialog box
Shift-Tab	Move to the previous option on a dialog box
Arrow keys	Move between options in a selected drop-down list
Spacebar	Toggle a selected option
Alt-letter key	Toggle an option using the underlined letter in its description
Esc	Cancel a dialog box. When a drop-down list or menu is open, ESC closes it instead.
Enter	Close a dialog box, accepting the default action suggested or any settings made
Alt-Spacebar	Open the System menu (with window commands like minimize, maximize, etc.). This is the same as right-clicking a window's taskbar button.

Table 24. Web keys

Key	Action
Ctrl-K	Insert a hyperlink
Alt-Left arrow	Go back one page (if available)
Alt-Right arrow	Go forward one page (if available)
F9	Refresh

Table 25. Cross-reference and footnote keys

Key	Action
Alt-Shift-O	Mark a table of contents entry

Table 25. Cross-reference and footnote keys (continued)

Key	Action
Alt-Shift-I	Mark a table of authorities entry
Alt-Shift-X	Mark an index entry
Alt-Ctrl-F	Insert a footnote
Alt-Ctrl-D	Insert an endnote

Table 26. Office Assistant keys

Key	Action
F1	Opens Microsoft Word Help (In Word 97–2002, F1 opens the Office Assistant unless it is disabled)
Alt-F6 and Ctrl-F6	Cycle through open documents
Alt-Down arrow	See more topics
Alt-Up arrow	See previous topics
Esc	Close an Office Assistant message or a tip window
Alt-N	Display the next tip in a tip window
Alt-B	Display the previous tip in a tip window

Table 27. Task Pane keys (Word 2002 and 2003)

Key	Action
Ctrl-F1	Close and reopen the current task pane
F6	Move to a task pane from another pane in the program
Ctrl-Tab	Move to a task pane when a menu or toolbar is active (from pressing F10 or Alt)
Ctrl-Spacebar	Open the menu of task panes while the taskpane is active
Alt-Home	Go to the Getting Started task pane (the one that opens by default when Word starts)
Alt-Left arrow	Go back to the previous task pane (if available)—same as back button
Alt-Right arrow	Go forward to the next task pane (if available)—same as forward button
Down arrow or Up arrow	Move between choices in a task pane

PART IV

Word Resources

This part lists Internet sites that offer resources, updates, tech support, tips and tricks, and various utilities for Microsoft Word.

Internet Sites

Microsoft's Official Office Site
Official news and articles, plus tips and tricks.

http://office.microsoft.com/

Office Update
Microsoft's update site for Office, which includes service packs, security patches, program updates, and new add-ins.

http://office.microsoft.com/officeupdate/

Microsoft Help and Support
Valuable technical resources for all of Microsoft's products, including a searchable Knowledge Base with thousands of how-to and tech support articles on Word.

http://support.microsoft.com/

Woody's Watch
Woody Leonhard's advice, news, and newsletters on all Microsoft Office products, including Word.

http://www.woodyswatch.com/

Word's Most Valued Professional (MVP) Site

> Home to the members of Microsoft's Most Valuable Professional (MVP) group for Word, this site contains FAQs, tutorials, downloads, and other useful information.
>
> *http://word.mvps.org/*

Word Newsgroups

> Microsoft runs a news server that hosts a number of Word-related newsgroups. You can read the newsgroups using Outlook Express, or Internet Explorer 5.0 or later. The news server is *news://msnews.microsoft.com* (or just *msnews.microsoft.com* if you are configuring it in your newsreader); the Word newsgroups all start with *microsoft.public.word.*

Microsoft Template Gallery

> Microsoft offers templates for all of the Office products, including Word.
>
> *http://office.microsoft.com/templates/*

Word Tools

Amazon Research Pane

> An add-in task pane that lets you search the Amazon database for book (and other product) information. Once you find a book, you can quickly insert a footnote, a product picture, or the product details into your document. Free download available.
>
> *http://www.amazon.com/gp/associates/research-pane/ download_rp.html/104-2490312-0238357*

CDEV Word Tools Bar

> This toolbar lets you update fields, insert random text, get addresses from your Address Book, display table cell references in the status bar, and more. Free download available.
>
> *http://www.cdev.co.uk/utils.htm*

ClickBook

A printing utility that lets you print customized day plan-ner pages, wallet booklets, brochures, and more. Free trial available.

http://www.bluesquirrel.com/ClickBook/

CrossEyes

This powerful utility lets you see a complete visual map of everything in your Word document, including direct formatting, styles, breaks, frames, etc. Free trial available.

http://www.levitjames.com/

Editorium Tools

This site features a number of productivity-boosting tools that let you automate various document manage-ment functions. Some are free; some are not.

http://www.editorium.com/

PureText

PureText lets you copy information from one source (e.g., a web page) and paste it into an application such as Word without all the formatting and HTML code. Free download available.

http://stevemiller.net/puretext/

Shortcut Organizer

Add-in for copying custom keyboard shortcuts between documents. Free download available.

http://www.chriswoodman.co.uk/Utilities.htm

Stylizer

This style utility lets you quickly reformat, fix, and apply styles to documents in as little as three mouse clicks. Free trial available.

http://www.levitjames.com/

WOPR

WOPR (Woody's Office Power Pack), created by Woody Leonhard, includes a large collection of Office utilities, add-ons, features, and enhancements designed to make you work faster and smarter. There is no free trial available.

http://www.wopr.com/

Word Key

A standalone utility that recovers all types of passwords for Word documents. A free trial version lets you recover passwords that are two characters or less.

http://www.lostpassword.com/word.htm

Word Pipe

WordPipe takes all the hard work out of replacing text across multiple Word documents. Just run WordPipe across your file server or web site to fix all affected documents in one hit. Free 30-day trial available.

http://www.crystalsoftware.com.au/wordpipe.html

Index

Symbols

* (asterisk) wildcard character, 138
.bmp files, 135
.doc files, 10, 135
.dot (template) files, 10
.emf files, 136
.gif files, 135
.htm/.html files, 135
.jpg/.jpeg files, 135
.mcw files, 135
.png files, 135
.rtf files, 10, 135
.tiff files, 136
.tmp files, 11
.txt files, 10, 135
.wmf files, 136
.xml files, 135
< (less-than) wildcard character, 138
> (greater-than) wildcard character, 138
? (question mark) wildcard character, 138
@ (at sign) wildcard character, 138
[ ] wildcard character, 138
^& wildcard character, 140
^p wildcard character, 139
{ } wildcard character, 138
¶ (paragraph mark), 22, 25
  selecting with paragraph, 50

A

/a startup switch, 136
accepting changes, 125
adaptive menus, 5
address book, using for envelopes, 112
alignment
  of paragraphs, changing, 54
  of tab stops, 55
  of table cells, 100
  using tabs, 7
  vertical, changing, 41
Amazon research pane, 156
anchors
  floating objects and, 18
  Object Anchors option, 67
  viewing, 19
animation
  cursors, 113
  turning on/off, 53
ApplyHeadingX command, 133

We'd like to hear your suggestions for improving our indexes. Send email to *index@oreilly.com*.

numbered lists (*continued*)
    creating, 62
    disabling automatic
        creation, 31
    removing numbers from, 133
    restart numbering, 63
numbering of captions,
        changing, 79

O

objects
    adding captions to, 78
    anchored/unanchored, 18
    creating, 94
    embedding in documents, 94
    floating, 18
    framed, 18
    inline, 17
    inserting, 86–95
    linking to files, 94
    manipulating, 92
    text with, 19
    (see also pictures)
Office Assistant feature, 114
    keyboard shortcuts for, 154
Office Clipboard, 51
Office Update web site, 155
Online Collaboration
        feature, 122
Online Layout view, 9
opening documents, 34
optional hyphens, inserting, 110
organizational chart,
        creating, 88
orphan/widow control, 70
Outline view, 9
outlining, keyboard shortcuts
        for, 151
Outlook
    contact list, 110
    sending documents to, 120
OVR button (overtype is
        on), 10, 48

P

page breaks
    forcing, 70
    manual, 69
    preventing, 69
    selecting/moving/deleting, 24
    showing in document
        window, 69
page orientation, changing, 40
paragraph marks, 22
paragraph styles, applying
        formatting using, 57
paragraphs, 22–24
    formatting, 54–56
        keyboard shortcuts, 147
    indentation of, changing, 54
    removing bullets/numbering
        from, 133
    selecting, 49
    styles, 24–26
passwords, locking documents
        with, 121
pasting
    copying and, 51
    Smart Cut and Paste, 29
permissions, restricted, 38
personal information, removing
        from documents, 32, 37
picture placeholders box, 68
    changing settings for, 32
pictures
    changing color settings, 93
    changing cropping for, 93
    inserting into documents, 88
    (see also objects)
pointer
    changing to command
        button, 134
    locating, 43
    moving, 133
pop-ups, disabling, 32
Portable Network Graphics
        files, 135

translating selections and
documents, 106
translation tools, 109
TRK button (track changes is
on), 10, 124
two-sided pages, printing, 41

U

unanchored objects, 18
Undo command (Ctrl-Z), 28, 48
Unicode text files, 135
Use wildcards option, 137
user information, changing, 114
user templates, 16
default locations for, 140
utilities for Word, 156

V

version compatibility, 121
versions of documents, 35
vertical alignment of pages,
changing, 41
vertical lines between
columns, 70
vertical rulers
adjusting headers/footers, 74
turning on/off, 67
vertical scroll bars, 42
viewing
comments, 123
markup, 124
page and other breaks, 69
views in Word, 9
changing, 65–69
Visual Basic Editor, 130

W

/w startup switch, 137
watermarks, setting, 65
Web discussions, 128
Web Layout view, 9
options in, 67

web pages
keyboard shortcuts for, 153
previewing documents as, 68
setting options for, 114
web text, adding for objects, 93
What's This? feature, 56, 74, 115
widow/orphan control, 70
wildcards and find
codes, 137–140
windows
controls for, 6
keyboard shortcuts for, 152
Windows bitmap files, 135
Windows Enhanced Metafile
files, 136
Windows Metafile files, 136
wizards
creating letters, envelopes, and
labels, 110
default locations for, 141
Woody's Watch web site, 155
WOPR (Woody's Office Power
Pack), 158
word counts, calculating, 109
Word for Macintosh files, 135
Word for Windows files, 135
WordKey utility, 158
WordPerfect Help, 115
WordPipe utility, 158
workgroup templates, 16
default locations for, 141
workspaces, shared, 122–123
wrapping styles, changing, 93
wrapping text
around objects, 19
around tables, 100

X

XML features in Word, 107–108
XML files, 135

Z

zoom levels, choosing, 68